Children's

MEDiA

YEARBOOK

2016

The Children's Media Yearbook is a publication of
The Children's Media Foundation

Director, Greg Childs
Administrator, Jacqui Wells

The Children's Media Foundation
P.O. Box 56614
London W13 0XS

info@thechildrensmediafoundation.org

First published 2016

ISBN 978-0-9575518-6-2 (paperback)
ISBN 978-0-9575518-7-9 (digital version)

Book and cover design by Jack Noel

Children's MEDiA YEARBOOK 2016

EDITED BY

TERRI LANGAN & **KATE DAVIES**

The Children's Media
FOUNDATION

MAKING IT HAPPEN

LOOKING BACK

LOOKING FORWARD

INTRODUCTION

ANNA HOME

—

The Children's Media Foundation: keeping the children's audience at the forefront of the debate around Charter review and the future of funding for kids' content in the UK

This year, CMF's activities have been dominated by the long debate over the BBC Charter and how to respond to the government's proposals. A Green Paper was published in July 2015 and other documents have been published subsequently, including the Clementi report on the governance of the BBC.

The Green Paper, unusually, contained two specific references to the children's audience – essentially officially accepting that there is "market failure" as evidenced by Ofcom reports from as far back as 2007 and proposing, in the briefest of terms, some solutions.

On one hand, the need to "protect" the children's budget at the BBC was floated. The Green Paper also included a reference to "contestable funding" – money that might be taken from the Licence Fee and distributed to other organizations to stimulate more content for children. Both of these proposals needed to be considered in the context of a secretary of state (John Whittingdale MP) who is generally in favour of a smaller, more "public service" BBC that intervenes in the market far less, but for whom children's content is a cornerstone of BBC public service. CMF can claim some success in lobbying the secretary

of state in his previous role as chair of the Culture Media and Sport Parliamentary Select Committee, so he understands very well the failure of the commercial public service broadcasters to commission anything of significance and the collapse in spending on UK children's content anywhere other than the BBC.

However, these two Green Paper proposals caused concern. The idea that the government would in some way "protect" a specific budget at the BBC seemed to us far too much like direct interference in the work of the Corporation. Our basic position is that UK kids deserve a well-funded BBC that can independently create children's content it can wholeheartedly stand behind rather than having its hand forced by regulations or spending quotas.

Equally, the idea of "contestable funding" was connected in the Green Paper with what has become known as the "top slicing" of the BBC's budgets to redistribute the money to other bodies, or companies. This, it seems to us, does very little to alleviate the real issue behind the market failure – that millions of pounds of commissioning money have been diverted away from children's content because the commercial PSBs are no longer required by regulation to provide children's programmes. We need to find new money to bring the level of spend back to what it was ten years ago, not move the existing pot around.

So our response in the various public consultations that have followed the Green Paper has been clear:

- No more cuts to the Licence Fee
- The BBC should itself commit to increasing the children's budget to accommodate new content for under-served audiences such as the over-tens while maintaining the range and quality of its existing services
- The government, having accepted that there is market failure, should now

conduct in-depth research into alternative methods of financing a contestable fund (with no raid on the Licence Fee). The research should also encompass how that fund might be organized and who might receive the funding – especially given the rapid changes in the way content is being distributed with all the new video-on-demand players in the market such as YouTube Kids, Netflix, Sky Kids and the proposed BBC iPlay platform.

CMF has stimulated public discussion of these issues. We kicked off with the debate we sponsored at last years Children's Media Conference in July 2015. This featured Alice Webb, director of BBC Children's, in her first public outing, with culture minister Ed Vaizey and representatives from Ofcom, Animation UK and CMF. Media commentator Steve Hewlett chaired a lively, informative and entertaining session.

In the autumn the consultations flowed in quick succession: from DCMS, the House of Lords Communications Committee, the Parliamentary Select Committee on Culture Media

and Sport, the BBC Trust, and Goldsmiths University, which staged an inquiry chaired by Lord Puttnam. All our responses can be found on the "Action" pages of the CMF website.

And the consultations continue. As I write, we have just responded to another House of Lords consultation – this time on Channel 4 and it's future.

In the same period we met and brokered more general meetings with many key people and organizations: Tony Hall, the BBC Trust, MPs, opposition shadow ministers, senior civil servants at DCMS and other organizations with whom we share concerns. We have spoken at the Westminster Media Forum on several occasions and on radio and TV.

In September we staged another public debate in London, this time with the ominous title "Staring into the Abyss". The debate brought out the differences of opinion between interested groups as to the best way to achieve more funding for UK kids' content. There are those who support top-slicing to achieve a fund and there are those who don't – the CMF included. To find common ground, the CMF arranged a meeting with Pact, the VLV and

Animation UK. The outcome was a joint statement on the future of BBC Children's, urging the BBC to commit to invest at least 8% of its overall content budget on children's content, with a minimum spend of £100 million.

More recently we suggested, and took part in, a round-table meeting with John Whittingdale to discuss how children's content fits in to the Charter renewal debate. We ensured that the partners in the joint statement were represented, plus a number of independent producers. All the relevant issues were discussed, including the pros and cons of contestable funding and the CMF proposal of a new alternative fund for content production. I wrote a letter to John Whittingdale after this meeting, reiterating our position. The letter can be found on our website along with our general policy statement.

This story is not finished yet. As I write this in May 2016, we await the publication of the White Paper later this month that will outline the government's conclusions on the BBC following all the consultations. There will be a brief window for further responses and in that period the CMF will organize a major event in London – a meeting of the All Party Parliamentary Group on Children's Media and the Arts (to brief MPs and Peers on the issues) – followed by a debate at the Children's Media Conference in Sheffield.

This is possibly the most important issue to face the entire children's media industry in the last ten years. The outcomes will be swift and potentially far reaching. There is every possibility that the government's agenda for the BBC may have adverse affects on the quality and range of content that the audience are offered in the future. Equally, with vision and care for the consequences of their decisions, politicians could make changes that stimulate the UK children's content market in exciting new ways. New money could be provided for production, reflecting the new platforms that are hungry for original and innovative content.

The CMF has been, and will continue to be, at the heart of the debate. We will press on with our proposals for an independent, well-funded BBC that supports and even expands its kids' content, and a new independently financed fund that stimulates real competition and growth in content delivery for the audience. It isn't easy for us to keep up this level of activity. We are a tiny organization with part-time staff supported by a few terrific volunteers. Our campaigning and lobbying takes place in the context of our events programme, the All Party Group, research initiatives, newsletters, press responses, our support of the yearbook and our development policy in other areas, such as internet security or the future of children's and family film.

This year has really stretched the CMF, but we have kept up. However, to continue – and be quite sure, there will be a need for us to continue – we need to raise more funds to keep the organization afloat. Please consider whether you or your company could become supporters. Details of how to do this are available on the CMF website, or from our fundraiser, Esther Fox: fundraiser@ thechildrensmediafoundation. org.

We believe that we can and do make a difference. But we can't do it without your help. ☺

"YOU STARTED IT!" ONLINE PIRACY – WHO'S REALLY TO BLAME?

CHARLOTTE JONES

Can the next generation of consumers really be considered different in their behaviour towards free content, or are they simply continuing a train already in motion? I remember older family members proudly telling me about the delicate art of timing a tape to record the top 40 chart from the radio, and taping films from the TV onto VHS cassettes. Piracy clearly goes much further back than Gen Zs, who could very well argue, "You started it!"

When I was young, one of our neighbour's children asked if we wanted any DVDs, as her dad was selling them "on the cheap".

At the time I didn't think that was OK, and I was worried her dad would go to prison. But skip forward ten years to my time at university, and finding free (and illegal) content online was just what we skint students did; it was normal.

My own experience certainly mirrors research we've conducted looking at piracy and content sharing among 6–18 year olds. As young people gain independence and begin to think in less black-and-white terms, their opinions begin to change. If "everyone" is sharing content and no one is explicitly telling them not to, surely it can't be wrong?

For digital brands, a key challenge is delivering a proposition that is considered valuable enough to pay for.

Thanks to the proliferation of social media and sharing platforms, young people are used to accessing content free of charge and have come to expect it. Why would they pay for something they can find for free?

This leads us to question: Have we created a generation of "innate pirates"? And if so, what does this mean for digital media brands?

If Gen Zs *are* innate pirates, does this make them a more challenging audience than previous generations?

Our research has identified that when children first start exploring online content, a lot of their experiences are orchestrated and controlled by their parents, and they are also taught what is "OK" and "not OK" to do online at school. The 6-8 year-old-age group are *content and guided* – they usually only experience content they're guided towards, accepting what they are offered without questioning it. As children get older (aged 9-11), they begin to stop taking their parents at their word and become *curious developers* of their own interests. Yet often they will still run things by their parents or echo things they think their parents want to hear. It's aged 12–14 that things really change – these *aided discoverers* have access to social media at a much younger age than any previous generation and encounter a wider network of peer influencers, who have a real effect on their moral compass. Young teens proactively share login details and specific links to content, and they also recommend websites and programmes to watch. Sharing links to media content online appears to peak at this age; it tails off as young people become *independent online consumers* (aged 16–18), confident in their own abilities and knowledge. By this time they have developed a sense of self and, while their friends are still important, they know their own minds and have become adept at finding and accessing content for themselves.

Sharing and use of pirate content has become normalized behaviour.

Having conducted in-depth interviews, traditional focus groups and Google hangout sessions with Gen Zs of varying ages, it's clear that by the time young people reach 16–18 years of age, using pirate sites is normalized to the point where it's routine; it's not even seen as cool or edgy. Evidence shows that 16–18 year olds treat pirate sites the same way as "official" sites (e.g. BBC iPlayer) and that pirate sites are often their first port of call as a "one-stop shop" for content. Gen Zs are adept at navigating past pop-ups and banners and don't find the layout of pirate sites off-putting. They know the sites work, they know what they want to watch and they know what to click on to access it. Deprivation exercises, such as blocking the route to their favourite source of content, are overcome easily. Young people know that if their favourite pirate site disappeared they'd have other options. They've become skilled but passive pinchers.

"Lots of people are sharing content and using pirate sites online, so it can't be an issue, surely?"

Key beliefs amongst young people that underpin this nonchalant attitude to pirating are:

- They are "consumers not posters" so they feel blameless and are therefore shameless in their use of pirate sites. "It wouldn't be me who got into trouble. It would be the person who put up the video in the first place."
- They are "creators not compilers". Apps like musical.ly and Video Star or sites like YouTube allow young people to share personal content with others online. "If I'm willing to share, what's wrong with consuming content others have put up?"
- They shouldn't have to police themselves. For young people, the internet means independence, and they don't think they should have to change how they use it. "If content is there, it's there to be consumed. It's up to regulators to take it down."
- They won't get caught. There are no top-of-mind examples of people receiving the same consequences for stealing content online as they would for stealing something "in real life". Therefore, availability bias leads them to conclude that nothing bad will happen to them. "Viewing pirate content

online doesn't feel like stealing. There's no obvious victim and it's a lot more socially acceptable."

"If I paid for media content that was available free online, people would think it was weird."

Young people have less money at their fingertips than older consumers and don't want to pay for things unless they have to. One young person told us, "I'd rather buy something physical like clothes or make-up than pay for music when I don't need to." But another key reason why people don't pay for media content is that they would be seen as "weird" if they did. They would stand out. We tested a scenario about buying a CD or a DVD in-store, and it quickly became apparent that young people have no desire to do that when there are cheaper, quicker and easier ways to access content online such as via YouTube. Many of them question why older generations spend money *unnecessarily* on one-off movie purchases. In a survey we conducted among 16–24 year olds we found that 40% of have never bought a DVD and 49% have never bought a CD, a percentage that is probably only going to climb.

"I'm not taking what isn't there to be taken."

We asked Gen Zs to respond to a number of hypothetical scenarios to test how they would respond when the opportunity to participate in illegal activity was presented to them. Having told them that their responses would remain anonymous, we asked if they would add food to their bag as they moved away from a self-scan till if they were hungry and couldn't afford to pay for it. Most firmly responded "no".

They are, however, opportunists, particularly in the less tangible, less "real" digital world. Tell them that an online retailer has a glitch in their system that means they can't tell whether people have returned an item or not and 65% say they would take advantage of this. They don't see this as stealing – they see this as smart. Tell them about a new website that has lots of films on it that have yet to be released and 72% would pay it a visit. Similarly, 75% of those who don't have access to Netflix at home would "definitely" borrow a friend's login details.

Embracing piracy and content-sharing behaviour can have a positive impact for a brand

Rather than passively waiting for information to come to them, this is a generation that wants to make things happen. We asked 150 16–18 year olds who they are inspired by, and "bloggers" was one of the top three responses. We also asked which brands they found most inspirational and they listed a stream of social media brands. Why? Because these brands ask young people to engage with them.

It is crucial for brands to build the right type of relationship with young people during their transition from "children with pester power" to "grown-up consumers". The worry for brands is that this next generation of consumers is so used to getting content for free that they'll resent

having to pay for it as they get older and they'll continue to look for ways to circumvent the system. However, our research has shown that for one brand in particular – Netflix – there could be an opportunity to use this "naughty behaviour" to their advantage. Among those who aren't currently paying for Netflix, 68% would be willing to pay for it in the future.

Has embracing log-in sharing by young people actually created a band of loyal brand affiliates for Netflix? Has exposing young people to their content enabled them to convert these viewers into fully fledged adult consumers once their piracy phase is over? It's certainly something for digital brands to consider; embracing piracy (or at least not clamping down on it) may actually help to engender long-term brand loyalty. Amazon recently launched a service called Amazon Video Direct to compete with YouTube, a brand that has long been ahead of the curve in embracing the next generation's desire to post and make money from their own content. The Amazon model looks to hook consumers in with a free online platform while exposing them to paid-for Amazon Prime content and services. It will be interesting to see how the piracy story develops as brands start to take more control and seek to meet the next generation on their own terms: "Yes, we started it, but now we're going to use it to our advantage." ◉

CROSS-GENERATIONAL ENTERTAINMENT

PETER ROBINSON

—

In this age of on-demand, anywhere entertainment, children have choice. Yet, in over 12,000 responses from kids who were asked about their favourite entertainment, the top ten brands stand tall. This could mean one of two things:
1. There is less choice than we perhaps believe
2. That there is choice, but the top brands stand tall because they do something special.
We believe both are true.

Seventy-five per cent of British children say it is hard to find new content (diagram one). Despite the proliferation of devices and on-demand entertainment, the removal of schedule actually makes it hard for some children and parents to find, trust and adopt new content.

The top brands (diagram two) don't instantly look as though they have much in common. But there is a pattern: all of the brands are either:

- Brands that were loved by parents or even grandparents in their childhood, and then passed down to kids
- Interacted with by both adults and children
- Respected by adults, used by children.

This paper presents our research on how the greatest children's entertainment brands should be appreciated across generations, and how to achieve that objective.

Methodology

This paper is sourced from three of Dubit's research tools:

- Dubit Trends, a global tracker of 2–15 year olds' and their parents' media consumption, with at least one country per continent. An online survey of over 12,000 2–15 year olds and 12,000 parents from February 2015 to April 2016
- Dubit PlayLab, a dedicated children-and-parent testing facility for toys, digital and video
- "Media-sorts", a warm-up task conducted during in-home immersions allowing children to show us their favourite toys, games, shows etc.

We also quote other clever works that we love and that

Diagram one: how often do kids get frustrated trying to find content?

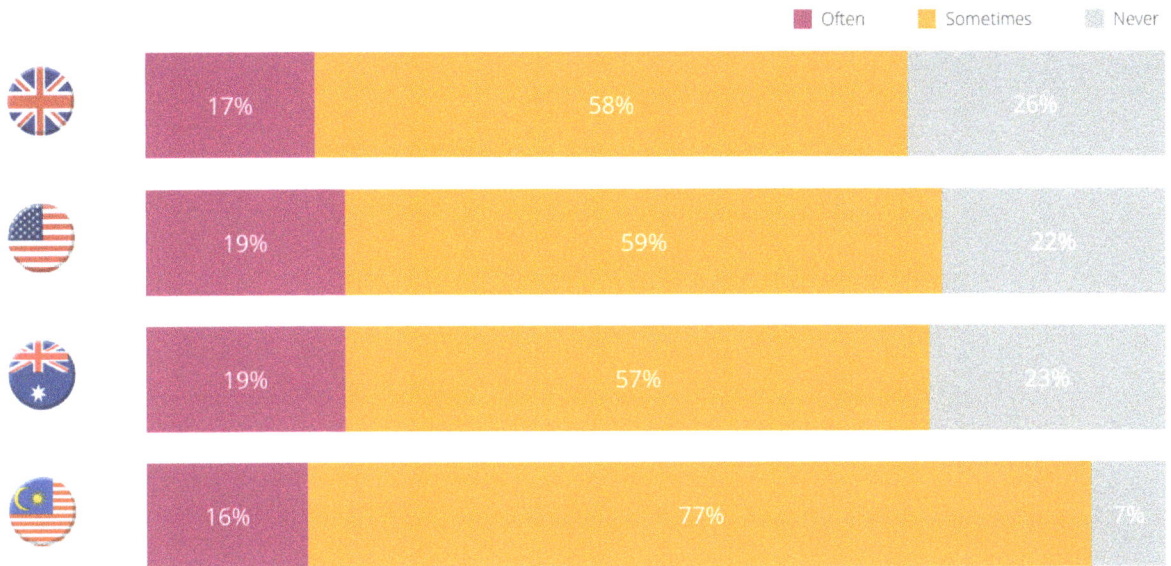

Legend: Often | Sometimes | Never

Country	Often	Sometimes	Never
UK	17%	58%	26%
USA	19%	59%	22%
Australia	19%	57%	23%
Malaysia	16%	77%	7%

Diagram two: top ten brands

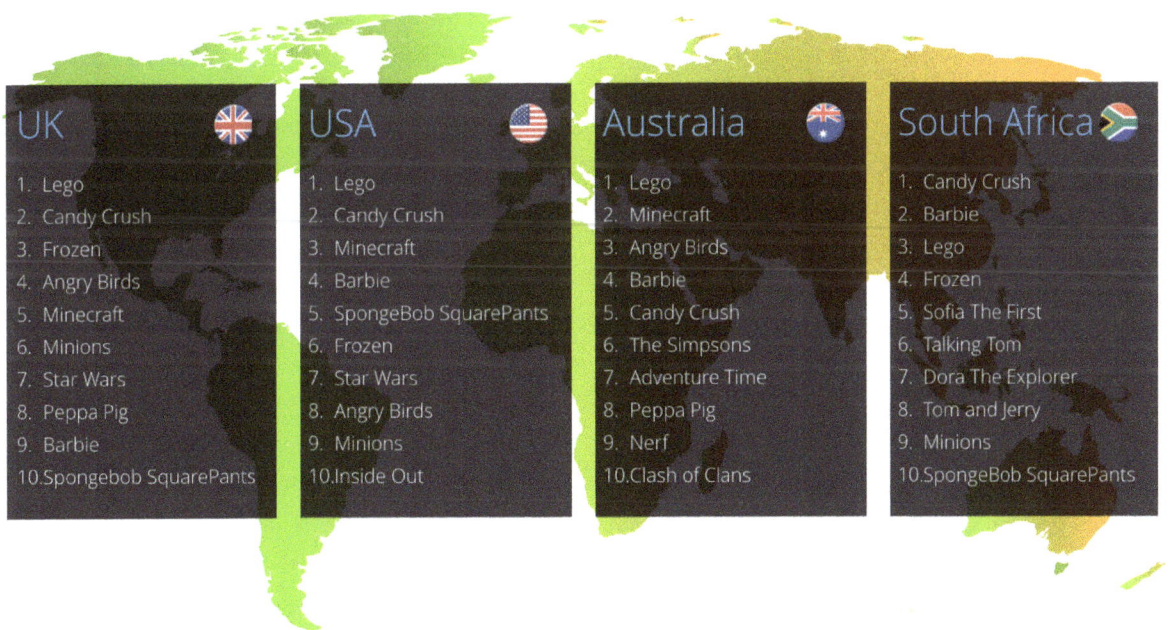

UK
1. Lego
2. Candy Crush
3. Frozen
4. Angry Birds
5. Minecraft
6. Minions
7. Star Wars
8. Peppa Pig
9. Barbie
10. Spongebob SquarePants

USA
1. Lego
2. Candy Crush
3. Minecraft
4. Barbie
5. SpongeBob SquarePants
6. Frozen
7. Star Wars
8. Angry Birds
9. Minions
10. Inside Out

Australia
1. Lego
2. Minecraft
3. Angry Birds
4. Barbie
5. Candy Crush
6. The Simpsons
7. Adventure Time
8. Peppa Pig
9. Nerf
10. Clash of Clans

South Africa
1. Candy Crush
2. Barbie
3. Lego
4. Frozen
5. Sofia The First
6. Talking Tom
7. Dora The Explorer
8. Tom and Jerry
9. Minions
10. SpongeBob SquarePants

offer a valid perspective.

Interactive entertainment

During Jeff "Swampy" Marsh's (*Phineas and Ferb*) keynote at CMC in 2013, he spoke about the importance of jokes going over a child's head and reaching the parent. The parent laughs, the child asks why, and they laugh together. It's a tried-and-trusted formula that has forged some of the most iconic and long-lasting kids' TV shows. Around the same time, I encountered GiggleBug, run by CEO Anttu Harlin, which also promotes "infectious giggling". These two brands – one already great and one hopefully on its way – are both trying to "make people interact".

I spend my life trying to spot patterns in piles of data; how simple it would be if there was only one metric that mattered:

Objective One: Encourage child and parent interaction
Objective Two: Make it happen over and over.

The common perception that children move away from their parents as they age is, in some respects, true. They become increasingly autonomous in their decision-making, many surpass their parents' competence on modern platforms, and peers become their main influence. But autonomy is managed (diagram 4), as we found with one 12-year-old boy who sat uncomfortably as his mum admitted to us that he still collected the *Beano* (which sat discreetly in his trusted place, under the bed). He was autonomous, but his mum still knew everything. He knew that she knew and, perhaps most importantly, he didn't mind.

Media sorts allow children to physically present their media universe to us. We are then able to discuss in detail how they consume their favourite brands. They lend a fascinating insight into how a child chooses and organizes entertainment across platforms. There are two consistent trends that appear during this exercise, across all types of home:

1   There is a space in every child's bedroom for gifts bought for them, or handed down by grandparents and parents. It's a treasured and organized space, often a bookshelf. In the UK, it will include books by Roald Dahl, C.S. Lewis, and Jacqueline Wilson, among others.
2   Lego and Monopoly will be present, and nearly always linked to family time.

Emotional scheduling

According to the media sorts, emotion plays a huge part in how children retain passion for a piece of entertainment. Social and emotional development walk hand in hand and are driven by modelling of those closest to the child – parents, grandparents and other adult carers. So it is hardly surprising that children's favoured entertainment brands – those with which they feel most emotionally connected – are often multi-generational.

When we ask children and parents the one thing they want more of, they say time together. Sadly, family time comes at a high premium in many households. A study published by Hollywood Bowl in March 2016 suggested that families spend 38 minutes together each weekday, four minutes longer than a study by Highland Springs found in 2015. This falls roughly in line with our own data. Entertainment accounts for a sizeable proportion of that 38 minutes; regardless of the platform, it drives family time. Here are two frequent situations we have uncovered:

Diagram four: children's level of autonomy from their parents

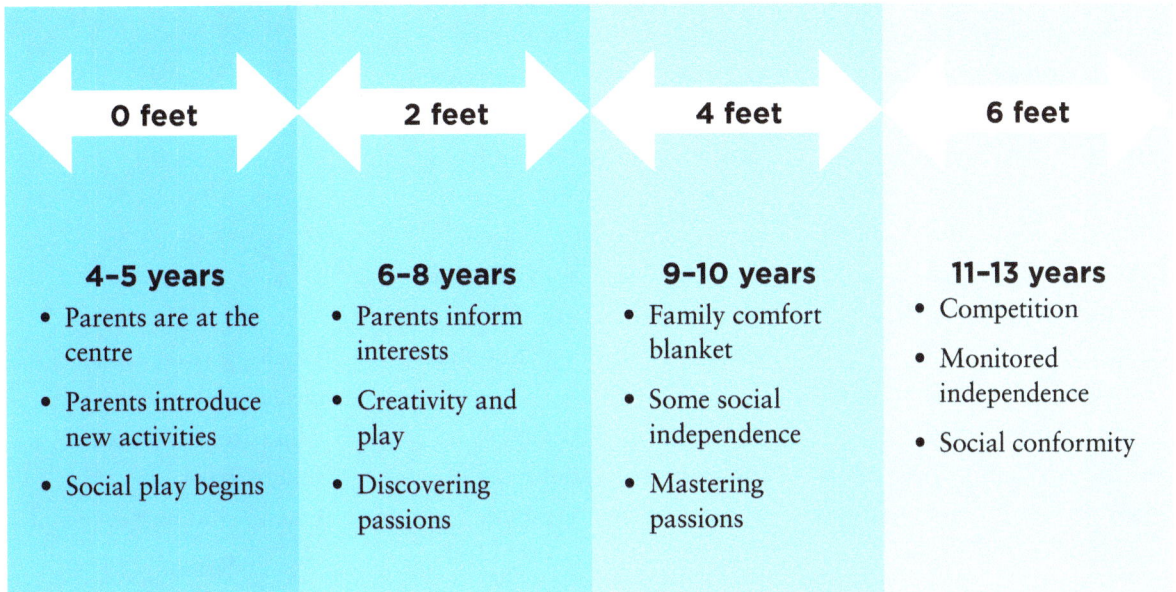

← 0 feet →	← 2 feet →	← 4 feet →	6 feet
4–5 years	**6–8 years**	**9–10 years**	**11–13 years**
• Parents are at the centre	• Parents inform interests	• Family comfort blanket	• Competition
• Parents introduce new activities	• Creativity and play	• Some social independence	• Monitored independence
• Social play begins	• Discovering passions	• Mastering passions	• Social conformity

Some families use screens for bedtime stories. Regardless of the platform, parents and children are in the same room and sharing "chill-out" time, with only specific brands allowed

While smaller screens are, if anything, more isolating than a room-serving screen, mobile media gets passed around. Quite often, parents and siblings share smart devices, collaborating on Minecraft or competing on Angry Birds.

Fifty years ago, the same study would have seen books dominating bedtime and board games dominating social gameplay.

Case studies

As part of this study we spent time looking at three of the top five brands among children. They all follow the set rules:

- Lego has been loved by many generations and continues to be a platform for play and development across the ages
- Candy Crush is played by children, parents (usually mums) and grandparents (usually grandmothers)
- Minecraft is loved by children and respected by parents, despite bemusement at its graphics.

While there are many reasons why each product is multi-generational, we have focused on one element unique to each brand.

Lego has been a staple of every child's development for 77 years, but when sales dipped, it evolved into a licensing machine and became a dominant force. The licenses themselves couldn't have been more ideal. Each one (Star Wars, Indiana Jones, Marvel, Harry Potter and DC) has an almost identical superfan audience – Lego "geek dads" (and mums) and a fiercely passionate young following. But when we ask children who introduced them to any of the above licenses and Lego, nearly three-quarters of the time it was a parent or older relative. Lego's essence of imagination for all ages has not changed, but the context in which that essence is delivered has adapted through its narrative to the modern audience.

We often talk about essence when nurturing a heritage or new brand. In this age of cross-platform brands, rapid licensing and increasing discovery networks, it is essential that each add-on doesn't just make money but sustains the core objective of the brand.

Candy Crush was not the first brand we considered as multi-generation entertainment. For the last year, Candy Crush has scored well among 2–15 year olds. But, according to King (the game's creator), its core audience is women aged 25–55. Rather than daydream, people today turn to their smartphones for distraction. Candy Crush provides that in a simple two-minute maintenance play or a substantial two-hour Sunday afternoon session. It also provides quick wins and progress, a reward that any human brain likes. Candy Crush

increases in complexity and difficulty, but its randomness and the simplicity of play means that there is always progress and reward. And that appeals to both young and old. Candy Crush is not exclusive: anyone can play, so we often meet eight year olds who have assisted their grandparents to overcome a tricky level. That's akin to what Jeff "Swampy" Marsh set out to do.

Minecraft has almost too many successful traits to mention, but one quote from a dad stood out: "I feel guilty asking my son to stop playing; he's in the middle of an accomplishment. I'd be mad if someone did that to me." How many parents would say that about a TV screen? Parents don't have to *like* everything their children watch or play, but they should respect it. Minecraft is one of the few apps, outside of the preschool market (Toca Boca, Duck Duck Moose etc) that parents truly trust to inspire their children. ▶

5

top tips for cross-generational success

1 Employ a really simple mechanic that aligns with a human motivation, e.g Candy Crush

2 Extend your narrative and core objective through complementary partnerships and licenses, e.g. Lego and *The Gruffalo*

3 Become a place that parents trust will have positive benefits to their children, e.g. Minecraft

4 Focus on a key metric for success and measure only that – don't become blinded by too much data, e.g. Gigglebug

5 Most importantly, design experiences that harness relationships between children and parents, even if it's one tiny point of interaction, e.g. all of the above.

THUNDERBIRDS ARE GO: CREATING FEMALE CHARACTERS IN ADVENTURE ANIMATION

ANNA POTTER

UK children's television plays a vital role in national cultural representation and community cohesion, entertaining and socializing its young viewers as they learn from the societal norms and values they see portrayed on screen. Children's television also creates a sense of place for its audiences, reflecting familiar situations, accents and locations back to them. Conversely, television from other parts of the world, often made with high production values, can expand children's horizons, teaching them about cultural differences and introducing a sense of a global community.

But what happens when some of the societal norms and values in children's television are unpalatable, or reinforce tired stereotypes while eschewing diversity? And how much responsibility does the children's TV production industry have to try to effect social change through the television it produces and distributes? The industry's acknowledged difficulty in ensuring diversity in its own workforce also raises questions about its capacity to ensure onscreen portrayals of diversity for the child audience.

In 2007 a worldwide study into gender representations in children's television revealed some interesting statistics about the genre in the UK, at a time when 68% of it was home grown. The findings showed

A female technician in ITV's reboot of *Thunderbirds Are Go*

that despite women making up 51% of the population, 63% of all onscreen characters were male, voiceovers in children's TV were generally provided by males, actors portraying female characters were more often thin – indeed, 40% were very thin – while males were more often overweight, 73% of all onscreen characters were Caucasian and a minuscule 1.2% had a disability.

Globally the situation was no better – on average, 68% of main onscreen characters in children's television were male. Where storylines were concerned, heroes in children's television also tended to be male. Female characters most often appeared at home or at school, while male characters were generally portrayed outside or at work.

Although more recent data is hard to obtain, many working in the industry are striving for greater diversity in the children's television they make, including more balanced gender representations onscreen. ITV's high profile reboot *Thunderbirds Are Go* provides a useful lens through which we can see how contemporary creative teams are subverting stereotypes in action-adventure animation while managing the myriad demands of producing children's television for global markets.

Part of the retro appeal of the original

Thunderbirds series lies in the ways in which it reflects 1960s social norms, despite being set in 2065 with science fictional narrative structures. Such norms include plenty of smoking and drinking, a utopian view of technology, having five men as the lead characters around whom most of the action revolves and the representation of the series' two key female characters as an ultra-glamorous socialite and a grandmother.

The 2015 *Thunderbirds Are Go*, a co-production between ITV Studios and New Zealand's Pukeko Pictures, targets an audience of 6–12 year olds. Executive producer Estelle Hughes believes that for animation particularly, increased female visibility is integral to more balanced gender portrayals, suggesting, "It's about seeing more female characters onscreen and seeing them doing jobs that are still being given to male characters, such as pilots, mechanics, drivers and crime fighters." Girls tend to move away from action-adventure animation at the age of around eight or nine, and Hughes was aware that creating compelling female characters that would engage girls in the new series made commercial sense.

The revamping of the Supermarionation original for contemporary audiences included the use of CGI animation and a cut in running time for the new episodes, from 44 to 22 minutes, with a concomitant adjustment in the pacing of storylines. Despite the need to improve female representation in the new series, the creative team felt that changing the gender of the five lead characters would

be a mistake; alterations to the Tracy Brothers line up were therefore vetoed at an early stage. As Hughes explains, "When you look at those five characters in the puppet series and their relationship to their specific five vehicles, it's a brilliantly created, worked-out series where those five characters and vehicles really complement each other and create a perfect whole. So that was the reason we retained the five male leads – creatively they worked. And they'd spawned an amazing series and brand that didn't need fixing."

In order to achieve more gender balance while retaining the five male leads, the creative team behind *Thunderbirds are Go* adopted two strategies at the writing stage. First, they reworked key female characters from the original series. Second, they used each episode's requirement for new characters in need of rescue to incorporate more females, particularly in roles that would have been cast as male in the first iteration of the show. Indeed, Hughes describes her starting point when talking about the writing of a new episode as "Why can't that character be female?"

For example Tin Tin, the daughter of Jeff Tracy's manservant Kyrano in the original series and renamed Kayo in *Thunderbirds Are Go*, provided an excellent opportunity for redevelopment. According to Hughes, "Kayo was a fantastic character to start from scratch with, as the original Tin Tin hadn't really stood the test of time." Kayo is now head of security for International Rescue, a capable and feisty young woman who wants to be proactive by going out and preventing crimes and thereby reducing the need for rescues. Her methods, which often include breaking longstanding International Rescue rules, cause her and Scott Tracy to clash repeatedly.

Kayo, who is deliberately dressed in a uniform of plain combat trousers and T-shirt with her hair pulled back in a pony tail, is also a non-combative martial arts expert whose superior skills mean she trains the Tracy brothers in physical and self-defence. She has her own vehicle, Thunderbird Shadow (although this is for stealth missions rather than rescues). Kayo's character has proved immensely popular with boys and girls and, says Hughes, "clearly demonstrates that you can have strong female physical action characters and boys will still completely relate to them."

The introduction of new characters that need rescuing due to technological disasters provided another means of including females in non-traditional roles. Many of those being saved from disaster are operating, designing and testing equipment, thus the high numbers of mechanics, miners, machinery operators, scientists and pilots associated with the technology gave the producers ample opportunities to incorporate female characters into these non-traditional roles.

ITV Studios were also supportive of *Thunderbirds Are Go*'s efforts to create strong female characters and provided sufficient resources to cast high-profile guest actors such as Jenna Coleman and Emilia Clarke in series two. As Hughes observes, the media attention this kind of casting generated provided additional opportunities

to distribute non-stereotypical images and increase female characters' visibility, in this case Emilia Clarke as an oilrig worker and Jenna Coleman as a geologist.

Nonetheless when introducing new female characters into rescue scenarios, there was a risk that the narrative structure would be based on active male characters rescuing passive females. As Hughes acknowledges, including more female roles while avoiding the trap of repeatedly creating damsels in distress was a delicate balance. The writers were, however, able to ensure that technological failures rather than individual incompetence created the need for rescue. As a result, Hughes notes, the rescued workers are nearly always "bright, competent, capable, impressive professional people, so making those characters female is absolutely worthwhile and valuable."

Clearly, consumer products remain a crucial component of contemporary animation production funding, and their success is vital to the sustainability of series such as *Thunderbirds Are Go*. Historically, however, a division has existed between boys' and girls' toys, including in the ways in which they are marketed. *Thunderbirds Are Go* has been able to subvert that norm to an extent, through the toys created by UK manufacturer Vivid and a further 75 global licensees of consumer products associated with the brand.

The range of toys accompanying the reboot includes not only Lady Penelope's iconic pink Rolls Royce but also new items such as a Kayo toy and vehicle, designed by Japanese visual artist Shoji Kawamori,

Kayo in *Thunderbirds Are Go*

whose credits include the *Transformers* toy designs. As a result, in many toyshops the merchandise is not confined to specific girls' or boys' aisles but sit in a mixed range, with *Thunderbirds Are Go* toys the second highest selling new licensed toys in the UK in 2015.

Any reboot of a cult classic is an ambitious undertaking. Nonetheless, *Thunderbirds Are Go* has been a commercial and critical success, with generally very favourable reviews and consolidated viewing figures of three million for its UK launch. With the production of a third series recently announced and a distribution deal in place with Amazon Prime in the UK and US, ITV's decision to reboot one of Gerry and Sylvia Anderson's best-loved series is clearly paying off. The ability of the creative team to include more balanced gender representations obviously resonated with contemporary audiences as well, contributing to the series' success.

Despite her commitment to onscreen diversity, Hughes accepts that when producing animation, the integrity of the storylines must be any producer's priority. Particular stories or episodes will require particular characters, which will entail individual judgement calls. But as she says, when making those judgement calls regarding the inclusion of female characters in children's television, "you absolutely have a duty to work through the why not?" Hopefully the next batch of research into diversity and gender representation in children's TV will provide more evidence that the willingness of creative teams like those working on *Thunderbirds Are Go* to challenge longstanding gender stereotypes is paying off.

ANIMATED Women UK

Supporting women in VFX and animation

WOMEN IN ANIMATION

LINDSAY WATSON

Having gathered a number of statistics on behalf of Animated Women UK and as part of my own Masters research at Bournemouth University, I was shocked to discover a continued lack of consideration for the female audience within the animated TV market.

Animated Women UK found that women in Britain's animation and VFX industries enter jobs at a lower levels than men, get paid less, get promoted less, hold fewer lead technical/artistic roles, and leave the industry earlier than men, often without having had children.

I believe this has a trickle-down effect and explains in part why there are so few female animated characters on free TV. My MA research found that girls aged 6+ want to see power, expression, confidence, self-acceptance and femininity in the female characters they watch. Empowerment, communication and uniqueness were also at the top of the list, and they want to watch shows covering topics such as nature, maths and science.

Is this what they are getting? Unfortunately not. I compiled a list of 87 animated series featuring a cast with at least one female lead that are currently showing in English internationally. Results indicated:

- Most series are 2D
- They are split almost equally between all-female casts and those with just one female lead
- They are mostly either dramas or comedy dramas, though a few are comedies
- Most dialogue is recorded using American accents.

Children also said they wanted to see characters that appear naturally human, with realistic bodies and waist sizes. As an industry we are letting them down, instead providing them with images that could be harmful to their health.

While some of the largest providers of girls' content – Disney and Mattel, for example – have moved in the right direction, and online shops such as A Mighty Girl have launched, selling specialized products that meet girls' needs, more can still be done. Companies like Hasbro, PGS, Lagardere Active, POP, Teletoon, Cartoon Network, Studio 100 and Mondo have indicated they are interested in making changes in this area – but for now, girls are still being excluded. For example the UK's CBBC website features eleven animated series with male leads, four with a mixed-gender cast and none with a female lead.

Broadcasters may argue that girls start watching live-action shows at an earlier age, or that they haven't responded well to animation in the past, but perhaps this is because they haven't had content developed specifically for them.

Academics, child experts and parents all have views about what girls should be watching, but its important for the girls themselves to be given a voice. More research needs to be commissioned and more content tested to find out which formats appeal to them.

Disney's *Frozen* has shown how successful content featuring female leads can be at the box office. It's about time our industry tried harder to understand female audiences. We need to let go of our fears, be brave and start innovating. Girls deserve what boys have had for generations – fun, engaging shows promoting self-belief and independence.

MINDFULNESS AND CHILDREN

DR BARBIE CLARKE

———

"The Stress Reduction Program became my lifeline it literally saved my life. One can find peace and calm in the middle of chaos and confusion."
Participant at the Mindfulness Stress Reduction Course, University of Massachusetts

Those of us working closely with children, either therapeutically, as teachers or as researchers, are keenly aware that children have different ways of responding to certain situations. What might be a deeply stressful situation for one child can be brushed off by another. Psychoanalysis has taught us that past experiences can profoundly affect the way in which we behave and respond to certain situations. Some children live with chaos and confusion in their lives but mindfulness is the process of learning to work with our attention in a different way. Building resilience and coping mechanisms is now recognized to be as important to children's learning as literacy and numeracy. In December 2014, Nicky Morgan, secretary of state for education, announced that "character skills" would be introduced to the curriculum with a multi-million pound push to place England as a "global leader" in teaching character, resilience and "grit" to pupils. Schools and organizations that offer activities promoting character in pupils will see programs expanded through a new £3.5 million fund, designed to place character education on a par with academic learning for pupils across the country. Teaching character skills may seem at odds with mindfulness, but it's not – many schools are choosing to adopt mindfulness training to help children cope with stress.

Why has mindfulness been adopted?

Concern about children's mental health is now high. The World Health Organisation has warned that mental ill health will be the biggest burden of disease in developed countries by 2030. The government has announced that it is investing £1.4 billion to transform mental health support for children and young people in England, with a £3 million pilot scheme to trial "single points of contact for schools to ensure support is joined up and quickly available when needed".

The theme of Children's Mental Health Week this year (8–14 February) was "building resilience" and teaching children to "bounce forward" from life's challenges. A report carried out by children's support service Place to Be and the National Association of Head Teachers found that one in five children will experience a mental health difficulty at least once during their first 11 years, and many adults with lifetime mental health issues can trace their symptoms back to childhood.

A report released in March 2016 found that 55% of 338 school leaders surveyed reported a large rise in pupils with anxiety and stress. This is partly because of children's apparent preoccupation with social media, but stress is also caused by exams and the constant testing of children from a young age. Almost 65% said they struggled to get mental health services for their pupils.

- 79% of heads saw an increase in self-harm or suicidal thoughts among students
- 40% reported a big rise in cyber-bullying
- 53% of those who had referred a pupil to Child and Adolescent Mental Health Services (CAMHS) rated them poor or very poor
- Overall, 80% of respondents wanted to see CAMHS expanded in their area.

Sir Anthony Seldon, former head of Wellington College and vice chancellor of Buckingham University, has called for daily "stillness sessions" in schools, saying a decline in traditional religious assemblies has left pupils with little space for reflection in the school day. He argues that exams become a problem when schools or parents put an "excessive weight" on them. "Psychologically healthy schools need not cost vast sums, and much can be done by heads changing their approaches, which will change the entire atmosphere throughout the school."

The UK may be leading the world in its recognition of the effectiveness of mindfulness and its recommendation for adoption. The UK mindfulness all-party parliamentary group published its Mindful Nation UK inquiry in October 2015. The group heard evidence from leading scientists, practitioners, commissioners of services and policymakers and sought to "address mental health concerns in the areas of education, health, the workplace and the criminal justice system through the application of mindfulness interventions".

It made rigorous, cost-effective suggestions for developing the potential of mindfulness. There is sound evidence to back up claims of the effectiveness of mindfulness. Mindfulness training has been shown to reduce the risk of relapse of recurrent depression by one third. A 2013 meta-analysis of 209 studies concluded that mindfulness-based training is an effective treatment for a variety of psychological problems, and is especially beneficial for reducing anxiety, depression, and stress.

The link between mindfulness and reducing children's stress is becoming apparent to pioneers in children's media. In 2015, Michael Acton-Smith, founder of Mind Candy and creator of Moshi Monsters, published the book and created the app *Calm*. In launching the book and app he explained the benefits he had gained from mindfulness and the way in which he felt it could support children.

What is mindfulness?

Florence Meleo-Meyer from the Mindfulness-Based Stress Reduction (MBSR) programme at the University of Massachusetts Medical Centre states: "Mindfulness is the *awareness* that arises when we pay attention, on purpose, in the present moment, non-judgementally."

Her colleague from the MBSR, Saki Santorelli, explains the notion of mindfulness thus: "We're living in the past or we're living in the future, but the past is gone and the future has not happened. The now is right *here*." Mindfulness, he explains, is "a way of being attentive to the present, to the activity of being alive, and, more importantly, participating in that act of being alive."

The widespread adoption

The history of mindfulness

While the teaching of mindfulness tends to be secular, the principles come from Buddhism, which for 2,500 years practised many of the techniques used by the mindfulness movement today. Its adoption began slowly in Europe and North America in the late nineteenth century, with commitment from the hippy movement in the 1960s and 1970s. A significant change came about in the late 1970s through the work of Professor Jon Kabat-Zinn at the University of Massachusetts Medical Centre. Kabat-Zinn had a PhD in molecular biology and was a committed Buddhist himself. He realized that his patients at the hospital might benefit from meditation and yoga, as their symptoms were often made worse by high levels of anxiety and stress. He and his like-minded colleagues developed the eight-week Mindfulness-Based Stress Reduction (MBSR) programme, and, as scientists, evaluated its effects, producing a substantial peer-reviewed body of research demonstrating that relieving stress and bringing about a reduction in anxiety could relive painful symptoms. The Stress Reduction Clinic has served as the model for mindfulness-based clinical intervention programs at over 200 medical centres and clinics nationwide and abroad.

of mindfulness might have come about through the sense that our lives are moving too quickly, that we are missing out on important experiences. Saki Santorelli explains, "Sometimes we look back a decade later and ask, 'Where was I for my children's growing up?'."

Many of us might share this sense that life is passing us by. In the recent Play Report (2015) that FK&Y carried out on behalf of IKEA in 12 countries with nearly 16,000 parents and 13,000 children and young people, 49% of parents said they felt guilty about not spending enough time with their children, and 73% said they would like to spend more time with their children. And their children had similar feelings. 51% of children said they felt their parents were always in a rush, and the same number (51%) said they would like to spend more time with their parents.

This sense of rush and "busy-ness" is undoubtedly exacerbated through the use of social media and what psychoanalyst Sherry Turkle, Professor of the Social Studies of Science and Technology at the Massachusetts Institute of Technology, describes in her book *Alone Together: why we expect more from technology*

and less from each other. In the Play Report, 23% of parents, 23% of 13–18 year olds and 17% of 7–12 year olds admitted, "Sometimes I only talk to my family at home through text messaging or social media".

Evidence that mindfulness can heal

Jon Kabat-Zinn's research at Massachusetts has been influential in the mindfulness movement. His research has "focused on mind/body interactions for healing, clinical applications of mindfulness meditation training, the effects of MBSR on the brain, on the immune system, and on healthy emotional expression while under stress; on healing (skin-clearing rates) in people with psoriasis; on patients undergoing bone-marrow transplantation; with prison inmates and staff; in multicultural settings; and on stress in various corporate settings and work environments."

In the UK a coalition of academic institutions, Oxford, Exeter and Bangor Universities, has created "The Mindfulness Initiative" to advocate for "a better understanding of mindfulness as a low-cost intervention and its potential in

a range of public services".

How does it help children?

As a relatively simple intervention, mindfulness is increasingly being adopted by schools. A US study published in March 2016 found that mindfulness improves children's brain functioning, which can affect self-regulation and facilitate academic success,

Another recent study with younger children in South Korea measured salivary cortisol levels before and after an eight-week mindfulness programme and found both relationships and behaviour were improved in school. Similar findings were found in a 2015 paper focused on children aged 9–11 in Canada, which also showed an improvement in social-emotional development. A US study published in 2015 found that 11 year olds with attention deficit/hyperactivity disorder (ADHD) displayed significant improvement in maths through a programme of mindfulness. Interestingly, an early study (published 2012) found that 8–12 year olds with ADHD benefited from mindfulness training when their parents also took part in parallel "mindful parenting" sessions.

Mindful parenting is a form of mindfulness training, described by Jon Kabat-Zinn as "paying attention to your child and your parenting in a particular way: intentionally, here and now, and non-judgmentally". Parents are encouraged to be aware of the present moment with their child, avoiding negative responses, paying attention to their child non-judgmentally. Daily meditation practice allows parents to find space and brings a sense of calm to the family.

Mindfulness is beneficial for children

Mindfulness, it seems, can positively alter a child's outlook on life. Evidence shows that it reduces stress and anxiety and can improve mental health outcomes as well as learning outcomes. Many blogs and websites are appearing that give tips on how to teach children to stop and take breath.

There is also growing evidence that mindful parenting can benefit both parents and children, allowing parents to disengage from emotionally charged stimuli, reducing their stress levels and enhancing their emotional availability towards their children, which in turn can help children's behaviour and anxiety.

Fourteen-year-old Anaya Ali, a student at the UCL Academy School in London, sums up her experience of learning mindfulness:

"The main reason mindfulness means a lot to me now is that I have moments when I can become stressed easily or over-think things. I go to my room, sit there and remind myself what my teacher would say: 'Focus on your breathing and be aware of what is happening now.' Once I open my eyes, everything seems to fix itself back into place somehow. I've been given advice like, 'Go and revise, it will clear your mind' or 'Do some school work', but none of it works as well as mindfulness. It gives people the chance to look at everything from a different perspective, a better perspective." ⊙

The UK all-Parliamentary report gives a good description of the process of mindfulness:

Typically, mindfulness practice involves sitting with your feet planted on the floor and the spine upright. The eyes can be closed or rest a few feet in front while the hands are in the lap or on the knees. The attention is gently brought to rest on the sensations of the body – the feet on the floor, the pressure on the seat and the air passing through the nostrils. As the thoughts continue, you return again and again to these physical sensations, gently encouraging the mind not to get caught up in the thought processes but to observe their passage. The development of curiosity, acceptance and compassion in the process of patiently bringing the mind back is what differentiates mindfulness from simple attention training. This practice can be held for a few moments as a breathing pause in the middle of a busy day, or for half an hour in a quiet place first thing in the morning.

What further research is being carried out?

Dr Mark Williams, Emeritus Professor of Clinical Psychology at the University of Oxford and director of the pioneering Oxford Mindfulness Centre until his retirement in 2013, is leading the Myriad study, funded by the Wellcome Trust. The study, launched in 2015, focuses on 11–14 year-olds because this stage of early adolescence is likely to be the age at which children begin to struggle with mental health difficulties. The £6.4 million research programme will be carried out by teams at the University of Oxford, UCL (University College London) and the MRC Cognition and Brain Sciences Unit, in collaboration with the University of Exeter, over seven years.

The first phase is recruiting teachers in secondary schools who will train in and teach the mindfulness curriculum to students aged 11–14. This is important; mindfulness cannot be taught by just anyone. Training is essential, and part of this training ensures that teacher practitioners experience and practice mindfulness themselves.

The three-part study includes the first large randomized control trial of mindfulness training compared with "teaching as usual" in 76 schools, which will involve nearly 6,000 students. The other parts of the study are a programme of experimental research to establish whether and how mindfulness improves the mental resilience of teenagers, and an evaluation of the most effective way to train teachers to deliver mindfulness classes to students.

Richard Burnett, co-founder of the Mindfulness in Schools Project, helped to devise .B, a mindfulness programme taught in secondary schools. Evaluation of the programme with a non-randomized feasabilty study included a total of 522 young people aged 12–16 in 12 schools that either participated in the Mindfulness in Schools Programme (intervention) or took part in the usual school curriculum (control). The trial provided evidence that among those taking part, stress was reduced and wellbeing was enhanced. The trial is being followed by Paws B, which is aimed at 7–11-year-olds, as it is felt there is less support for primary school children. Katherine Weare, Emeritus Professor at the Universities of Exeter and Southampton and co-author of the report, has also written about the advantage for teachers to take part in mindfulness training.

EXPERIENTIAL MARKETING

AMANDA GUMMER

—

Everything has an equal and opposite reaction – so said Einstein! And we agree. With increasing online marketing and sales activity, there is also an increase in demand for events where children can see, touch and play with products before (or even without) buying them.

At Fundamentally Children, we have found that parents and children very much like to "try before they buy". We haven't just heard this from the parents we speak to, we've seen evidence of it with the growth of family festivals and events such as 3foot People Festival, Kidtropolis and Play Fair. Toy companies are beginning to recognize the value of these events and digital companies need to keep up if they want to benefit from the opportunities on offer.

Simply providing lots of screens for children to play on won't work at a family event. One of the reasons parents take their kids to family festivals is to get them away from screens and you don't want to alienate the parents from the start. Deciding what will be on offer for families is where your brand is so important. By truly analyzing and understanding your brand values, messages and the play patterns children engage with when interacting with your products, it becomes relatively easy to translate your digital content into fun "real world" activities that captivate children when they visit your

Children and parents at the launch of Lil' Ocean Explorers, a new range of toys from Little Tikes

stand and increase engagement with your products.

The importance of providing children with a balanced play diet is being increasingly recognized by parents. Therefore, making sure your digital content has a life off the screen as well is crucial for the acceptance and longevity of your products and also provides a vehicle to reach out to children at live events, opening up a whole stream of marketing opportunities for your brands.

As well as introducing new children and potential customers to your brand, family events also create an opportunity for valuable consumer insight. It's a perfect market research situation and whether you simply observe, conduct a quick survey or set up testing sessions at the event, you can learn a lot from seeing how children and parents react to your products.

Another often missed and underrated opportunity is observing how parents respond to their children's reactions to your product. There's little good in a preschooler being crazy about your product if that causes the parent to be concerned about an addiction to screen time.

As children mature, parental approval is less important, but having the opportunity to talk to parents at events about their concerns and aspirations for their children is a cost-effective way of evaluating new products and kicking the tyres on those that have already launched.

ANIMATING THE HOLOCAUST

KATH SHACKLETON

—

The Holocaust. Genocide. Child refugees. Not the easiest of topics for animation. A new studio. Our first series. Even more tricky!

Fettle Animation is a 2D animation production company in Pennine Yorkshire. We were given the task of making the Holocaust relevant to today's young people, and we relished taking on the challenge.

Children of the Holocaust is an animated series based on real-life stories. We animated six elderly holocaust survivors' memories of their dramatic escape as children from Nazi-occupied Europe and the process rebuilding of their lives in the UK.

We worked with BBC Learning to produce the series. It was initially intended to be a learning resource aimed at 14 year olds studying the Holocaust as part of the National Curriculum in schools, but it soon grew into something far bigger than we could have ever imagined. Clips are permanently online in the UK at www.bbc.co.uk/programmes/p01zx5g7/clips.

Animation is a great way of putting complex subjects across onscreen. It can show abstract thoughts and emotions, tell stories for which there are no images, portray hopes, fears, dreams, aspirations and memories. It's a really condensed form of communication and can put across a lot of information in a short amount of time, telling difficult stories with wit and sensitivity.

We created *Children of the Holocaust* with Leeds-based charity The Holocaust Survivors Friendship Association, whose members are involved in widespread educational work. We recorded several hours of really moving interviews with six of their members and edited them into short clips.

A still from *Children of the Holocaust*

Fettle Animation's director, Zane Whittingham, designed simple digital cut-out characters to tell these stories, carefully researched from period photographs. We then worked to find age-appropriate ways to convey some of the brutality of the Nazis to our young audience without directly showing the full horror of what they did. We found powerful imagery in the political propaganda of World War Two: giant, brutish soldier figures picking up helpless, tiny people; animals symbolizing human behaviours; wartime insignia used as tools and weaponry. Zane referenced German Expressionist artists such as George Grosz, graphic novels such as Art Speigelman's *Maus*, and 1940s political cartoonists. This gave the project richness and a subtle humour and brought a fresh approach to a subject that people have encountered many times before.

We worked with Creative Skillset and their wonderful Trainee Finder programme, which gave us subsidised bright young graduates to work on our production. They worked on animation, backgrounds and as production assistants. Our trainees were excellent and the Skillset support came at a perfect time for our company, helping us to scale up to the challenges of our first series. We all worked tirelessly and learnt such a lot from one another during the process of production. Particularly successful were animator Ryan Jones, who now works permanently at Fettle Animation, and Oana Nechifor and Laura Tattersfield, who are now successful freelancers. Executive producer Helen Brunsdon helped us to plan out our animation production pipeline. Music was composed by The Composer Work's Paul Honey, who did an excellent job conveying the light and shade of the stories through music and gave added drama to

The team behind *Children of the Holocaust* © Olivia Brabbs Photography

our animations. Sound was by the Digital Audio Company's Dave Aston with online editing from Phil Bedwell at The Other Planet.

We also worked with executive producer Liz Molyneux and self-shooting director Tim Baxter to make short live-action interviews with the survivors reflecting on their lives today and why it is still important to talk about the Holocaust.

We got a great response from our first screenings of this work and realized how much interest there is around the world in the subject of the Holocaust. We went on to create a TV documentary,

combining the animated shorts and live-action interviews. This was broadcast on primetime BBC Four on Holocaust Memorial Day in 2015 and has been subsequently broadcast in ten countries worldwide including Australia, South Korea, China and Israel, thanks to our agent Sydney Neter from SND Films in Amsterdam.

We've had to all get new passports, as *Children of the Holocaust* has also appeared at ten festivals around the world – a full run from Chicago to Annecy. We've had lots of travel adventures! We've also had to buy ourselves a trophy cabinet: we've won a Japan Prize, the first ever Sandford

St Martin's Children's Award and two Royal Television Society Yorkshire Awards. We were also nominated for a Children's BAFTA, a British Animation Award and a BUFVC Learning Onscreen Award. We have really appreciated this recognition and the increased profile has been really helpful in building our company.

We were also one of the first companies to claim a UK animation tax break on this project. Thanks to the BFI and HMRC and all those involved in campaigning for this – it has made a huge difference to us as a small company and has given us the resources we needed to get our work out there.

We are now publishing a book, *Survivors of the Holocaust*, with Hachette Children's Books, a graphic novel based on the artwork from the films. It's so exciting to see our work in a different medium, and for our survivors to tell their stories to another new audience.

However, it's making a difference that matters most to us. We feel we've helped our survivors tell their stories to the wider world with power and dignity and to draw parallels between their experiences and the experiences of child refugees today. Young people can learn so much by watching the films, not just about a difficult period of history but also about why diversity and tolerance are so important today.

Here are the stories:

Ruth

Aged five, she escapes over the mountains from East Germany into Czechoslovakia. She is saved by the courage of her mother who travels perilously across Europe, arriving in England at the very last moment before war is declared.

Martin

Aged eight, he is marched brutally from Germany to Poland in the middle of the night by the Nazis in the so called "Polkenation". Escapes to England on the Kindertransport, only to experience the worst of the Blitz in Coventry.

Trude

Aged nine, she witnesses Nazi tanks occupying her hometown of Bratislava, Czechoslovakia. She is taken by her aunt to England but is lonely and struggles to settle there without her mother and father. As an adult, she is still searching for the truth about what happened to her parents in the concentration camps.

Heinz

Aged 13, his schooling and social life in Germany is affected by the rise of anti-Jewish laws. He gets caught up in the horrific events of Kristallnacht, a violent pogrom. He escapes to England, only to be interned by the UK government as an "enemy alien".

Arek

Aged 14, he survives the squalid conditions, hunger and cruelty of Auschwitz-Birkenau, but 81 members of his family and most of the Jewish population of his hometown in Poland are murdered. Forgiving the Nazis is impossible for him.

Suzanne

Aged six when the Nazis enter her parents flat. A neighbour rescues her and hides her under her kitchen table. Her idyllic Parisian childhood is snatched away from her and she is taken to live in hiding and work on an isolated rural farm. Neglected and forgotten, she is not rescued by the Red Cross until two years after the war.

The survivors in these films are incredible people who all have risen above their adversity. They have gone on to have families of their own and to achieve great academic success, stellar careers and positive involvement in their communities. They are all still active and healthy well into their 90s. They are warm, funny and have very distinctive personalities. They are generous with their time and all have enjoyed working with us on this project. They are our constant inspiration.

We'd like to thank everyone who has been involved in this project – there are far too many to list. They have shown dedication above and beyond the usual call of duty. We'd like to pay particular tribute to our commissioner on this project, the BBC's Katy Jones, who died suddenly and unexpectedly last year. Her energy and faith drove us forward on this project. She is very much missed.

We are so proud of the impact that this project continues to have. Thank you again to everyone who has been part of our incredible journey! What an awesome year!

CONTENT, DISTRIBUTION, DISCOVERY: THE ROYAL FAMILY

DAVID KLEEMAN

It's a truism that "content is king", but content without well-targeted distribution leaves a lonely kingdom. So, perhaps distribution is queen?

Even if you have both content and distribution, though, young people need to know how and where to find your content in today's anything, anytime, anywhere media world. Otherwise, the king and queen rule only themselves. So discovery is the ace that's requisite for a winning hand.

Once upon a time, discovery was simple. Television dominated and kids knew that some channels or blocks were programmed for them, especially at logical times: early morning, afternoons before the news, the iconic Saturday morning slot. The competition was two or three other TV channels, picking up a book or toy, or going outdoors. Today, especially as children spend increasing media time with tablets, *everything* is competition: kids are just a home button away from games, books, video, communication, exploration, learning and more.

How tough is it now? Dubit research finds that more than 60% of kids are often or sometimes frustrated trying to find content they want. Maybe they don't know what they're looking for; maybe they know what they want but can't find it in the content maelstrom.

There's good news, though, if you're lucky enough to get

Cross platform: top 10 properties

We are going to show you a selection of toys, games, apps, TV shows and books. For each one we'd like you to tell us how you enjoy them.

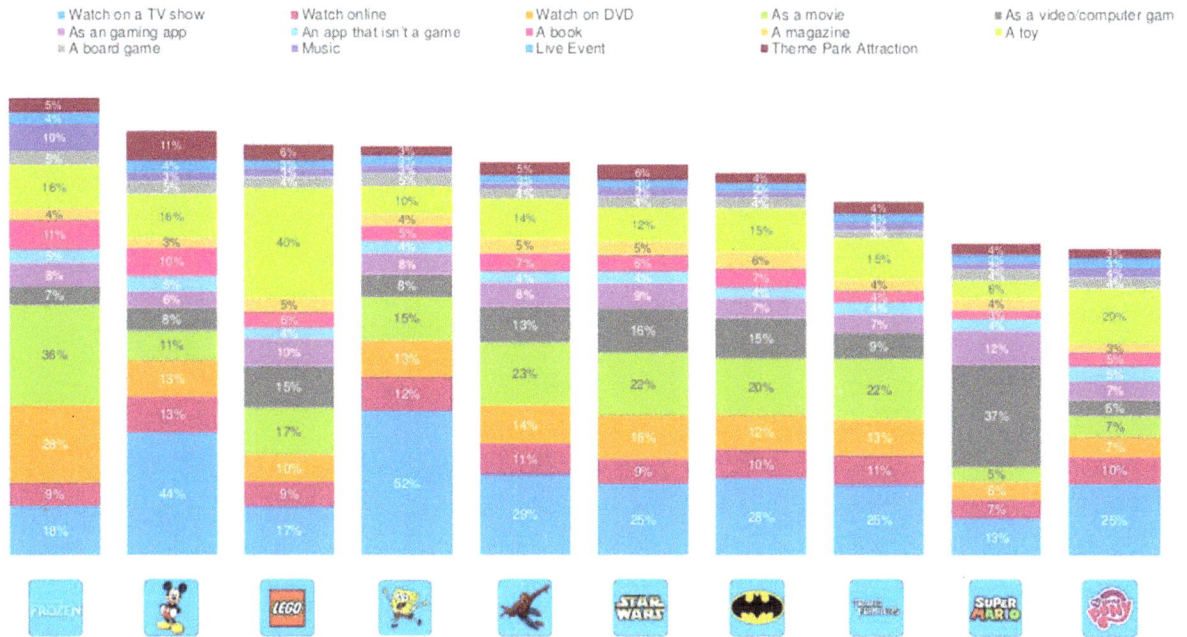

Legend:
- Watch on a TV show
- Watch online
- Watch on DVD
- As a movie
- As a video/computer gam
- As an gaming app
- An app that isn't a game
- A book
- A magazine
- A toy
- A board game
- Music
- Live Event
- Theme Park Attraction

found and adopted. Kids engage more deeply than ever with their favourite characters, stories and brands. They'll follow you across platforms, consume your content voraciously, and share it with others. ("Sharing" and "recommendation" complete the Royal Flush, to torture the metaphor.)

Here, then, are five thoughts on making content more discoverable and sharable.

1. Don't discount the ongoing value of live TV viewing

Some may say that live viewing is passé, but heed the story of ABC for Kids in Australia, which pulled _Curious George_ from its late afternoon schedule only to endure a barrage of letters from parents, accompanied by photos of crying children. Not in the children's realm, but the 2015 _Fear the Walking Dead_ premiere set same-night viewing records for a basic cable debut.

If you're on YouTube, consider releasing new content on a consistent timetable that kids can anticipate; if you're on a streaming service without a ready vehicle for scheduling, you might use marketing messaging to suggest fitting moments or moods for your brand.

2. Be cautiously multi-platform

Single-source distribution is becoming extremely rare; more common is an an anxious need to be on *too many* platforms. The chart on the previous page demonstrates how kids interact with their favourite brands in a wide variety of digital and physical ways; however, they also tend to associate a character or story *most* with one or two platforms.

You can go broke trying to be everywhere. Moreover, kids can sniff out a fraud and will reject content that's put on the wrong platform. Develop a world you can build broadly, but start with "sweet spot" authentic platforms for your audience and content. Drive discovery in those few places, then use your relationship with the audience to introduce new options.

3. Cherish your first fans

Dubit Trending finds that young people who consider themselves innovators or early adopters share their favourite things on a daily basis at double (US) or even triple (UK and Brazil) the overall population's rate. While the "first in" are the hardest to attract, they're also the fans that will determine your trajectory, from flash-in-the-pan rise and plummet to lasting long-tail stability.

Sharing on a daily or weekly basis appears to peak at ages 8–10, the time when divergence of personal interests really takes hold, when mastery is a big motivator and unique knowledge a big source of pride, and when many kids are getting their own mobile devices.

4. Don't ignore the tried and true

It's tempting to use the newest social networks to promote discovery. For some audiences or at some points in a brand's lifecycle, that may be very valuable. According to our tracker, however, kids and tweens still share their "likes" face-to-face at school or at play more often than digitally. Facebook makes its appearance as a top sharing method among 11–15 year olds, but live personal sharing still ranks very highly. Coming at the question from the other direction, TV advertisements are still kids' top source for hearing about brands, with friends second and parents (surprisingly, and not just among toddlers) close behind.

5. Know what drives your audience

The motivations that lead young people to seek and adopt new content and brands have remained fairly constant over the past 20 years, but the avenues they use to fulfill those motivations shift with technology. Innovators and early adopters are still characterized as risk takers, but now they seek the next new thing in niche, online communities rather than specialist magazines or from local trailblazers. Among the early majority, celebrity endorsement is still powerful, but young people's trust and modelling has shifted from TV and movie stars to YouTubers and other digital influencers.

It's like *Game of Thrones* out there for King Content. As difficult as it is to ascend to the throne, it's equally hard to stay there. It takes patience, insight and some luck to draw the Royal Flush – content, distribution, discovery, sharing and recommendation. I hope the five points above help you play your cards right. ⊙

This column appeared originally in *Kidscreen*.

APPS: THE NEW BATTLEGROUND FOR CHILDREN'S TV

STUART DREDGE

A year ago, there was one children's video app that really mattered: YouTube.

From toy-unboxing channels like Disney Car Toys to nursery-rhyme channels like Little Baby Bum and Minecraft gamers like Stampy, children were watching millions of YouTube videos – often on tablets or smartphones belonging to their parents.

More and more children are accessing media via mobile devices (including tablets). In November 2015, Ofcom published research showing that 53% of 3–4 year-olds and 75% of 5–15 year-olds now use tablets.

What's more, the percentage of 5–15 year-olds who watch television programmes on a tablet rose from 20% in 2014 to 27% in 2015, and the number who watch TV on mobile phones rose from 11% to 15% over the same period.

Children don't just use mobile devices to watch videos, of course – they're also playing games, using apps and, as they get older, using social networks like Snapchat and Instagram.

Unsurprisingly, this boom in mobile viewing hasn't gone unnoticed by the television industry. It has been a powerful incentive for the broadcasting world to place more focus on apps. A year on, YouTube has competition from the broadcast world in the form of BBC iPlayer Kids and Sky Kids. Even before the iPlayer Kids app launched, the BBC said that a third of show requests to its main iPlayer app were for children's shows. Meanwhile, Netflix has a dedicated Kids Mode in its

app, Amazon is commissioning original children's shows for its app, Disney has launched an app to stream its archive of TV shows and films and Angry Birds maker Rovio has launched a standalone app for its ToonsTV network of cartoons.

There are already some discernible trends in how these new children's video apps work. For example, they are all designed to be used by children with minimal parental involvement, with simple, clear interfaces and an emphasis on images, ensuring that even early readers can find their way around.

The apps are designed for parental oversight, however. Parents can download shows for offline viewing – a key feature, useful for long car, train or plane journeys – and they can create individual profiles for each child, tailored by age, so kids can't access inappropriate shows.

Business models vary. iPlayer Kids is free, while YouTube Kids is free and ad-supported – something that has caused controversy in the US, as the rules governing the separation of ads and content that apply to broadcast TV do not apply to YouTube. Sky Kids is free for Sky's subscribers – an incentive not to turn to another TV provider – while Netflix Kids is part of the monthly subscription to that service.

Meanwhile, DisneyLife costs £9.99 a month, Hopster £3.99 a month, and PlayKids £2.99 a month. It's not yet clear how willing parents will be to pay a standalone subscription for this kind of app.

How might these apps evolve over the coming years? The BBC has hinted at plans to open up iPlayer Kids to other providers. While the initial focus is likely to be on other broadcasters, it would be fascinating to see it integrate popular children's channels from YouTube too.

British startup Hopster has been very inventive, including simple educational games in its service. Each game reinforces the key themes of each show, and

children can access them after they've finished watching the relevant programme. For now, Hopster's bigger rivals are firmly focused on kids watching rather than playing, but it's possible some of them will bring in more interactivity – or at least add features to recommend relevant children's apps, which could be a boost to their developers.

The glut of children's video apps also highlights a wider trend: the blurring of boundaries between what we think of as "shows" and what we might describe as "short-form online videos".

The production values of a well-funded BBC or Netflix children's show may seem a world away from videos by Minecraft gamers like Dan "The Diamond Minecart" Middleton, vloggers like Zoe "Zoella" Sugg and nursery-rhyme channels like Little Baby Bum. But the production values of videos from top YouTube creators are rising, and some YouTubers are working within increasingly show-like formats – Stampy's educational science show *Wonder Quest*, for example, which was part-funded by YouTube. There's an argument that children don't care about production values, anyway: if they are more engaged by

watching someone building a Minecraft castle for half an hour than by an episodic TV drama, they will vote with their touchscreens.

In March 2015, 42 of YouTube's top 100 channels (by views) were aimed at children. Those 42 channels generated 10.3 billion views that month alone, according to online-video industry site Tubefilter's chart. Of those 42 top children's channels, only two belonged to traditional brands – Disney and Lego – while 20 were toy-unboxing and review channels run by YouTubers. YouTube is a world where a pre-school child called Ryan who stars in weekly toy reviews can generate 645.2 million views a month, where Little Baby Bum's nursery rhyme animations can get 492.4 million views, and where The Diamond Minecart's Minecraft adventures can get 337.4 million views.

The recent wave of children's video apps highlights the fact that the competition for kids' attention isn't just between Sky, the BBC, Netflix and YouTube. It's between the shows and talent of the traditional television world and the new digital stars and genres emerging online. ◎

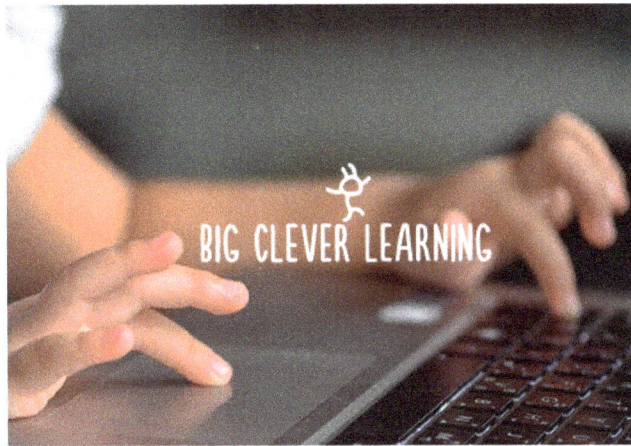

THE NEW ED TECH FRONTIER

JUSTIN COOKE

—

We all know that change is inevitable, but what are the key themes that are going to be driving innovation in ed tech?

We feel that there are a number of themes that we keep coming back to. Some of them aren't necessarily new (Virtual Reality has been around for almost 80 years), but as technology has evolved, so too has its potential in the classroom.

Virtual reality

Let's start with VR. If you haven't played with Google cardboard, you probably should. It'll cost you a few quid and an iPhone to get started. But the idea of using cardboard in VR is nothing new. Remember the View-Master, a cardboard disc with tiny transparencies that you placed in a plastic viewfinder? If you pushed the lever on the side, the View-Master would take you through a series of famous landmarks in 3D – almost as if you were there!

But in recent years, technology has allowed us to explore videos in 3D. At Sherston we've been looking at how we can use the available technologies to create an engaging experience for young

Big Clever Learning acquired Sherston in 2003

users. The technology that exists now is OK, but the emerging technology is going to be better – much better. And as costs come down, the potential to bring real-life experiences into the classroom and collaborate with others in a virtual world is really exciting, particularly for education content producers like us.

Internet of Things

IoT, as it's more commonly known, is any physical device that is connected to a network, allowing it to collect and exchange data. If you have Sonos to manage your music, or Hive heating controls at home, then you'll be all over this, and we've all read about cars that drive themselves. IoT technology is used by medical professionals, too, to track whether people have taken their insulin. But it's now becoming clearer how IoT might be used in classrooms. Pupils could control a physical object using code, for example. That would be a great way for children to see the physical impact of the theories they have learned. We like what the guys at Hackaball have been doing: their product encourages children to learn about computational thinking by writing code that makes a ball react to external stimuli.

Syncing up

It's only relatively recently that we've seen technologies syncing up. It used to be that you had your computer at work and the documents you were working on sat there on the server. If you had any software, such as Photoshop for design or Sage for accounting, it arrived as a CD-Rom and was installed on a computer. Now, for better or worse, our documents sit on the Cloud and can be pulled down via many different devices, whether we're sitting in the office or at the top of a mountain. You subscribe to software and get automatic updates. Synching is important in the classroom because it enables schools to collaborate with each other and links the classroom to the home. At Sherston we've spent a lot of time this year thinking about how we can use this technology to make it easier to share children's use of our products with their parents.

Assessment

Measuring attainment and progress is vital for all schools but it can be challenging for teachers to show that their assessments of pupils are accurate. We think that technology will play an increasing role in this, as our products will be able to track a range of subtle interactions to build up a picture over time. A teacher probably wouldn't be able to pick up on all of these interactions, given the number of children they are assessing and the limited amount of time they have to spend with each individual pupil. We will be able to provide teachers with evidence of their pupils' progress – greater accuracy or speed in completing tasks, for example – and help them measure progress over time.

Personalized learning

Personalized learning is nothing new, but it will continue to develop along with new technology. The right technology makes it significantly easier to tailor learning so that pupils of all levels are challenged an appropriate level.

Providing educators with a wealth of high-quality content and a seamless way of incorporating this into lessons should be at the heart of all educational technology propositions.

A LAND OF OPPORTUNITY – IF YOU CAN START LOOKING SIDEWAYS

ALEX CHIEN

China is a tricky subject – it's easy to lose track of what's going on in the kids' market, particularly when faced with overwhelming figures relating to population, online viewership, spending power, regional variations, the pace of change and so on. So I thought I'd share and break down some recent data to help readers gain a better picture of what's happening and how their own activities might integrate with the Chinese kid's market in the future. All numbers are approximate as of year end, 2015.

There are 170 million children under 12 in China, which equates to 23% of the total population (1.37 billion). Out of that 170 million, 25% are under two, 26% are aged 3–5, and 49% are 6–12.

There are over 300 TV channels in China, and more than 30 are kids' channels. Of these 30+ kids' channels, less than a fifth have the budget provision to acquire content and/or produce original content locally – and even then, the budget can be significantly less than a western producer or broadcaster would be accustomed to.

TV is still the preferred and most accessible viewing medium for kids, though viewing on mobiles is a growing trend due to the high penetration of smartphones. When kids watch content on smartphones, they're usually with their parents, though they're not necessarily co-viewing. PCs and tablets are the next most popular ways to view. Key OTTs/IPTV/ video streaming players are

用孩子的眼睛看世界

less strict environments to host acquired content, but again the numbers are far from most international or regional offers when it comes to kids' content, with box office hits being occasional exceptions. At the time of writing, Japanese anime *OnePiece* has 2.1 billion total series views, *Dora the Explorer* has 1.6 billion total views on iQiYi and *Peppa Pig* has 2 billion total views on YouKu. Compared to the audience figures you're probably familiar with, you might be thinking, "This is a goldmine!" And it is a goldmine, if you measure success by eyeball count, but less so if you measure the impact on your bottom line. This is because the price tag for content has nothing to do with the number of viewers, and a subscription revenue-split model is not yet the preferred practice in China.

In terms of transferring rating/viewership success to monetary return, distribution alone will never get you there, despite the increase of OTT platforms. China has never been a goldmine when it comes to content acquisition budgets in the kids' sector, and most buyers don't mind non-exclusive deals. The golden rule of L&M forming the lion's share of anticipated income also rings true here – if you have the right partners and strategy, merchandise will hit the shelves as soon as a new IP is introduced.

China's kids & family media landscape is indeed a land of opportunity – there's still a huge appetite for quality content, and slowly but surely, local producers are getting better at creating it. Parents and kids' consuming capabilities have also extended, from purchasing merchandise designed to sustain the "emotional connection" to a brand, to more immersive lifestyle or extra-curricula offerings. There are increasing numbers of ticketed indoor/outdoor play areas and theme parks available, as well as creativity/DIY tutorials; quality, contemporary online content matched by on-the-ground events; tours; and an increasing amount of subtle product placement and shop fronts that offer activities mirroring the content spread via social media. These marketing schemes are all tried and tested in other markets – they are not new innovations. Watch this space – transactions may be on their way to matching the viewing figures, but for the time being the Chinese are turning the ancillary into the main event.

Let's look at some research conducted with a sample of 100,000 families across China in 2015, published on Baidu. More than half of these families spent slightly over 30% of their total annual budget on their (in most cases) only child. Thanks to the recently implemented "two-child policy", this figure has the potential to rise. The biggest expenditure is on books (print and digital combined), followed by food and beverages, then toys. Education is the number-one draw for parents and the big publishers are well aware of this. Detailed research about family expenditure on education for 0–6s and 7–18s has been published by iResearch and is available online.

I was recently asked to advise on ways to transfer the ratings success of a top-rated animal show on a FTA channel to financial success. My analysis pointed towards the development of printed content as the best way to do this, but an alternative approach would be to consider launching a zoo- or vet-themed summer camp catering to the ever-growing number of middle class families who would do anything to give their children a unique first-hand experience. If there were fluffy toys in the gift shop on the way out they would sell too, but toys aren't the main area of growth in the current market.

THE PRIX JEUNESSE FOUNDATION: EMPOWERING CHILDREN AND INSPIRING ADULTS WORLDWIDE

ALISON STEWART

—

Prix Jeunesse means many things to many people around the world. Personally, the activity of this organization has opened my eyes, broadened my mind and given strength to my work. I would go so far as to say that Prix Jeunesse played a significant part in helping me get my current job in BBC Children's! I'll explain more later…

This introduction, from the Prix Jeunesse website, explains the ethos of the organization:

"The Prix Jeunesse Foundation is a world-embracing movement that supports and showcases high-quality television for children and young people. The aim is to promote content that reflects children's lives within their own countries and as part of the wider world, thus enhancing their own identity and instilling an understanding of other, diverse lives and cultures."

Year round, Prix Jeunesse engages producers, broadcasters, researchers, educators and young people in hands-on workshops, in-depth screenings called "Suitcases" and research partnerships. The Foundation's main activity is its renowned world television festival, Prix Jeunesse International, which has taken place in Munich every two years since 1964.

Research

The Prix Jeunesse Foundation conducts its own studies and also works in affiliation with the International Central Institute for Youth and Educational Television (IZI). In a research project in 2014 they tracked gender representation across 19,664 programmes with 26,342 fictional characters from 24 countries. This was the largest analysis of children's television ever undertaken.

Their current research deals with how children and young people between the ages of 6 and 19 perceive the current refugee situation. The aim of the project is to give producers and educators insight into how to report on this issue, and how to foster in young viewers an understanding of diversity and inclusion. Early research is showing that children who watch children's news content are much better informed, have less fear and have more positive feelings towards refugees than if they consume adult content on the subject or learn about the situation from adult conversation.

Prix Jeunesse International

Every two years, delegates from more than 60 countries meet in Munich for the Prix Jeunesse International Festival. At the time of writing, three weeks before the event, approximately 600 attendees have registered. The theme of this year's Festival is "What it means to be me: Identity and Children's Television".

The largest part of the Festival comprises screenings of the finalist programme entries, and participants vote for ultimate winners. There are also panel sessions, short info sessions and "Beyond TV" sessions for digital entries. Evening delights include the annual soccer match and the ever-popular Nordic Karaoke Night.

The Festival screens fiction and non-fiction entries for the following age groups: Up to 6 years, 7–10 years and 11–15 years. Each category screening is followed by moderated discussion groups, where delegates share their thoughts on prevailing themes, outstanding entries and controversial content (and there's always some controversy!). It's an opportunity to hear from some of the programme makers and to learn more from the delegates about their countries, cultures and opinions on children's media. These discussions are in depth and passionate, and the combined expertise of the children's media professionals who take part makes them unmissable sessions.

The Festival culminates in a prestigious awards ceremony, where the category winners are announced. There are also awards for cross-media and short form entries, a UNICEF and a UNESCO prize and the Prix Jeunesse "Heart Prize" for the entry which has most touched the heart, which is voted for by all Festival participants.

This year I was one of 12 international "preselectors". We met in January and between us we watched over 450 programmes in order to nominate the finalists in each category. A hard job, as we could only put through one in every five entries. By the time you read this, the Festival will have taken place, the categories judged and prizes awarded, so I can share a few comments from the preselectors' reports without prejudicing any results!

Preselector: David Kleeman, USA (Non-fiction, 11–15 years)

"I'm excited by the entries from the NHK/Japan because I love their creative visual approach. In particular, though, it's wonderful to see *Pythagora Switch* – a show

that won at Prix Jeunesse in the preschool category years ago – come back as a teen series, with the same clever approach to maths learnin, aged up for the generation that grew up on the series! One other show that will undoubtedly be controversial is *Puberty*, from NRK Super in Norway. It's more graphic than any sex education show I've seen before, but it's also important and successful in its straightforward and factual content.

The 11–15 Non-Fiction category was heavily populated with tough, issue-oriented entries. Self-discovery is a universal adolescent theme and the struggle of teens to find themselves is always present at the festival. With the Prix Jeunesse 2016 theme of "Identity," however, combined with the world events of the past two years, we saw a striking selection of stories around migration and youth refugees."

Preselector: Jan-Willem Bult, Netherlands (Fiction, 11–15 years)

"We watched programmes ranging from a fantasy comedy about Singapore school kids hunting ghosts to a realistic drama about the abuse of a British teen, from an Argentine story about integration to a Japanese folktale featuring the big bad wolf and the three little pigs on trial in a courtroom.

The screenings of the 11–15 Fiction category will make you laugh, shiver and gasp in wonder. Maybe you'll cry, and hopefully you'll feel uncomfortable sometimes, too. Prix Jeunesse International always celebrates diversity and introduces you to unknown places, languages, cultures and moral values. It sometimes challenges us and it always make us learn."

Preselector: Frederik Hansen, Denmark (Non-Fiction, up to 6 years and 7–10 years):

"There were many strong, well-made stories that relied on children to show and tell their reality. The programmes that stood out were the ones that trusted and gave room for the children to be authentic … but also outstanding were the programmes that made us smile and laugh and which sincerely wanted to bring laughter and joy to kids' lives.

The theme of "pushing boundaries" was very present in the programmes we screened, especially in the "Non-fiction, up to 6 years" category. There are a number of programmes this year that will result in very heated discussions on what is and what isn't appropriate content for pre-schoolers – but who could imagine a Prix Jeunesse without those very important discussions?"

Preselector: Alison Stewart (me!), UK (Fiction up to 6 years and 7–10 years):

"Our panel commented on the challenge of serving the 7–10 age group, who want to be "grown up" and yet need help coping with the more serious issues that life can present. The theme of this year's Festival is "Identity and Children's TV" and this theme was explored best in the entries where children made their own decisions when faced with dilemmas.

Many of the animated entries in the "Fiction, up to 6 years" category are deceptively simple programmes that deal with weighty subject matter. *Trude's*

Pet from Germany treats the subject of jealousy with humour and poignancy. *Lily's Driftwood Bay* from Northern Ireland addresses the subject of death with great sensitivity. And with *The Piglet who wanted to be a Bird* from Macedonia, it's all in the title – it's a search for identity and acceptance. To sum up this category: the programmes are for little people, but the themes are big."

Prix Jeunesse Suitcase

The Prix Jeunesse Suitcase is offered to adult professionals and children in the form of screening and info sessions. The Suitcase comes packed with the best and most innovative entries from each festival. Often it is combined with a training programme on a specific subject (e.g. script writing). In 2014 the suitcase made 30 stops in 20 countries.

David Kleeman is a regular "unpacker" of the Suitcase and he will present a session with highlights from the 2016 Festival at CMC in July. Here he explains the process:

"The Prix Jeunesse Suitcase is a great creative refresher. In the course of a single day, I can show over 20 programs or clips from more than a dozen countries – a "tasting menu" for those who can't make it to the full "smorgasbord" in Munich. While I always include some of the winners, I'm usually more excited about showing entries that are unlike anything the audience is likely to have seen, or those that have tried something bold. For each Suitcase, I try to tap multiple emotions – to amuse, to touch, to amaze, even to anger.

Being able to talk about the Suitcase programmes – to reach outside one's own experience and discuss them from the perspective of another culture – is a great muscle to exercise. Almost always, after a Suitcase, participants say they've gone back to work energized to take creative risks."

And David's word "energized" brings me back to my opening statement, that Prix Jeunesse helped me get my job! In 2010 I attended only my second Prix Jeunesse International (this year will be my fifth). Inspired by the screenings, invigorated by the discussions and hoarse after the Nordic Karaoke Night, I left the Festival a day early to attend an interview for my current role at the BBC. The Festival had reminded me why I work for the audience I have served for most of my career. Every programme I had watched in Munich, every conversation I had had there, all the insight I had gathered from the Festival's global perspective gave me a feeling of such pride and confidence in what we do as children's media providers that I almost danced through that interview.

As a disclaimer, you aren't guaranteed a wonderful new job if you attend Prix Jeunesse International! But you will be guaranteed an insightful, emotional and invigorating experience. Furthermore, the work done by the Foundation is as important and relevant now as it has ever been, at a time when appreciating difference and accepting diversity are critical skills that all our children need to learn. ◯

www.prixjeunesse.de

#TOYLIKEME

REBECCA ATKINSON

—

Since my last child was born six years ago, something else has bred in our house: toys. We started off with a few rattles, and as the years progressed the plastic proliferated into an army of Playmobil, a soup of Lego, a sea of Sylvanians. Just after my daughter's sixth birthday last year, I noticed something startlingly obvious about our toy box: not one plastic figure had a wheelchair, a hearing aid, a white cane or any kind of disability at all.

I have spent nearly 20 years working in TV production and print journalism (including at BBC Children's) and have always been interested in the way these industries represent disabled people, but this was the first time I had noticed the startling lack of representation in the toy industry. I took to the internet to see if I could find any disability representative toys. Google returned near empty searches, and what did exist was so boring and grey it spoke nothing but negativity to children.

Images from the #ToyLikeMe campaign

As someone who had grown up wearing hearing aids, I remembered firsthand how it felt to be a child who never saw themselves represented by the mainstream and what that can do to self esteem. I wanted to change this for generations to come and get global brands like Lego, Mattel and Playmobil to include representations of disability in their products.

The next morning I called on some fellow mothers, including former Ragdoll play consultant Karen Newell, who has a son with vision impairment. With their help we launched the online #ToyLikeMe campaign to call on the global toy industry to start positively representing disability and end the cultural marginalisation of 150 million disabled children worldwide.

I plundered my kids' toy boxes and starting making over toys to give them disabilities and asked other parents to do the same. Like a match to a firework factory, things went bang and within days our image of a Disney Tinker Bell doll with a model cochlear implant had gone viral with hundred of parents asking where they could buy it, prompting global press coverage.

Images from the #ToyLikeMe campaign

These parents were responding to what I call "the ping of recognition", a deep sense of identification experienced by someone in a minority when you see your experience reflected back at you in the cultural mainstream. It's the same feeling you might have if you were abroad in a foreign country, where you don't speak the language and see a stranger from your home country after months of travelling alone. You will most likely go up and talk to them, ask them where they are from, look for common ground, perhaps feel some form of instant affinity. This is what many parents of disabled children do too – look around for commonality,

people experiencing the same things as their children, things that will reassure them their children will be OK and will be valued by mainstream society. By marrying characters like Tinker Bell with the minority experience of having a cochlear implant, #ToyLikeMe creates shareable images which are propelled by that "ping of recognition".

"I showed my daughter your Tinker Bell picture tonight," wrote a follower. "Her mouth dropped and she said, 'This is me. This is so awesome!'"

#ToyLikeMe receives messages like this every day. There is a potency in showing a child with a difference (whatever that might be) a mainstream character like themselves. It's hugely powerful and affirming for that child to see themselves reflected positively in the cultural mainstream.

Since #ToyLikeMe was established a year ago, we've amassed over 35,000 followers in 45 countries, received support from Julia Donaldson, author of *The Gruffalo*, and comedy genius Stephen Merchant.

We've enlisted Playmobil, who become the first global toy brand to join our "toy box revolution" after more than 50,000 people signed our change.org petition calling on the brand to produce characters with disabilities like the ones we had created. The first in their range is due out later this year.

In January 2016 Lego unveiled their first ever wheelchair-using mini-figure at Nuremberg Toy Fair. The UK press attributed this product to #ToyLikeMe's campaign and the story was carried by global press and met with jubilation, proving that sometimes the smallest things can make the biggest impact. The significance of this move by Lego should not be underestimated. Children's industries – not just toys, but also books, TV, film and games

Stephen Merchant supporting #ToyLikeMe

The modified Tinker Bell doll with a cochlear implant

– really do have the power to change lives by changing perceptions.

For a disabled child, growing up as the only kid in your class or school to use a wheelchair or a hearing aid and never seeing anyone like you in the world around you can lead to a sense of isolation and low self esteem. Seeing yourself reflected by huge toy brands like Playmobil and Lego shows that these brands value you and believe that everyone should be included and celebrated, not just able-bodied children. But #ToyLikeMe doesn't advocate that disabled toys are just for disabled children. We strongly believe that *all* children will benefit from disability being positively but incidentally included across all children's industries. If we can create a more inclusive landscape in the media, then perhaps we can educate by stealth and change attitudes in the real world too.

DIVERSITY MEANS EVERYTHING

NATHAN BRYON, KARA SMITH AND GREGORY BOARDMAN

—

A producer's view

Having put heart and soul into the *Rastamouse* production, with all its positivity and warmth, it was upsetting for all of us involved to hear unfounded negative comments and even offensive remarks coming from individuals in business, and in the retail and licensing sectors, when asked to consider something that was a little bit different. Seeing children's reactions to the television show gives us an immense sense of satisfaction and witnessing the *Rastamouse* music and storytelling work in primary schools is thrilling, but undoubtedly one of the biggest pleasures has been watching the production become a beacon for new talent. Individuals have been inspired by the presence of *Rastamouse* on screen to make contact with us.

Taking the time to talk to these new voices and creatives from all kinds of backgrounds has brought home to us just how alienating our industry can be. Given the size of our company, it's impossible to employ or help everyone who has knocked on the office door, but by sharing their details with other producers and broadcasters we're able to make sure that the first chat might be a steppingstone to other opportunities. I have long believed that creative conversations can sometimes take years to come to fruition and a good conversation is never wasted. Over the next few months, the *Rastamouse* legacy will give rise to a new children's show that we hope will become another beacon for talent with new and different stories to tell. Yet no matter hard we try to ensure diversity onscreen and behind the camera, there is a sense that it's still not enough.

Take a look around the world and there are plenty of sobering stories that make it clear that diversity isn't just an issue for the media, though we need to take the media's impact on young minds seriously, both on a local and a global level. There's no doubt that our business needs to take the lead in ensuring that that existing roles and new opportunities are open to all, no matter where they hail from. However, if we want real diversity, the whole system, from top to bottom, needs to embrace radical and urgent change. To be truly diverse, we need to change how we work and change how we influence and encourage new talent – and we must re-educate ourselves. We need to change how each of us values knowledge; we need to change the knowledge that we value; and then we need to completely overhaul the way we measure success.

It's all too easy too slip into an approach governed by consumer- and business-orientated goals, but our models of business and our modes of living are the legacy of Western European thinking and they fail to provide us with a perspective that allows for real diversity. We ought to move away from the emergent notion of the media being a talent show, an incubator of narcissism, and look seriously at the socializing function of the things we make and do. Books, television and digital media are increasingly powerful tools that contribute to our lifelong learning. We may hope that our young audiences laugh *and* learn from the fruits of our labours, but adults and parents need to think about what we can learn, too. Only then can we make our business and our world a more inclusive place. If those of us working in children's media take the lead, then maybe corporations, politicians and other people in power may also take notice.

A writer-director's view

The importance of diversity is an issue that has remained ever-present in almost every industry. There are many social and commercial factors that contribute to the apprehension organizations feel when approaching the subject. However, it is especially galling that diversity remains an unresolved issue in the broadcasting industry if but for the single reason that broadcasting is built on the platform of storytelling. The old adage "two heads are better than one" is standard in the industry because production is collaborative by definition. So the idea of inclusion does exist – at least, up to the point of clarifying which "heads" will be called on for representation.

People often differentiate me from others in my profession by calling me a "diverse" writer. On the one hand, this statement is true; I have lived and worked outside of the UK, my educational background includes a mix of the arts and sciences and, of course, I am female. But calling me this also suggests that I am included *in spite* of my background, not because of it.

Children's broadcasting is a unique space because the stories, characters and ideas aren't anchored to social or political fundamentals in the way that other subgenres are. So it stands to reason that there is greater scope to include a diverse group of people behind the scenes and in front of the camera. To the BBC's credit, there has been a realization that there is a problem, and a flurry of diversity campaigns and programs has been launched. The disconnect, however, is that these programs focus the idea of diversity only on race. While this is a positive step, the concept of diversity implies a multitude of representation that goes beyond race to include gender, sexual orientation, language, culture, religious and political beliefs, education, profession and age.

It seems to me that the focus on race as the token diversity perspective has been divisive among professionals who just want to be identified for their talent and ability (you know, like all the other writers who don't have "diverse" as their status). The producers I've worked with have done just that, and it has been a truly amazing and fulfilling journey – but I know my experience is an exception, not the norm.

So what's the way forward? Simply to lead with diversity. No longer can the concept of inclusion be a bolt-on – it has to be fundamental, especially in an industry whose mandate is to guide, educate and entertain future generations.

A view from the writer, actor & part-time professional afro

When I was invited to contribute to this piece I was so excited and ready to vent, rant and shout about the lack of diversity in front and behind the camera, but writing this article has been a struggle and certainly more of a challenge than sitting in my PJs writing about pirates, unicorns and musical caretakers. As I started to type I realized how big and intimidating the subject is. Diversity to me means *everything* ... I live in a diverse environment, so it's all I know!

All races, sexes, abilities and social groups need to be represented, equally and fairly, in the media, but what's currently happening is insufficient and uninspiring.

Growing up in England, a young black boy attending a predominantly white primary school, I was one of the few kids who did not have satellite or cable. I asked my parents a million times before our family got Sky when I was 18, and I must have literally sat in front of the TV for a week when it arrived. So as a child, the television I could watch was limited by my circumstances – but more importantly, looking back at all the shows I watched, I never saw any onscreen diversity. I didn't even know what "off-screen" diversity was, but I imagine that wasn't in a good place either.

What's so damaging is that, as a child, you do not recognize the difference. If the white middle-class face is the norm, you don't think twice or question why no one like you is onscreen. The situation is the same in children's literature. Check out your local bookstore and look for a diverse children's book cover. The situation is alarming.

I have an Afro and my hair has always been different. Growing up, I couldn't understand why I didn't have the same hair as the young white kids in school, and the other children couldn't understand it either. Today I still meet adults who don't understand my hair and just want to touch it. A warning to all readers: this is a big no-no! My parents always explained my race and background to me, but I think as a young black boy trying to formulate an identity, life would have been easier if I'd been exposed to diverse stories, different cultures and religions in a safe and – most importantly – *fun* way. What is so magical about children's media is that it's about fun *and* education, but by not addressing diversity we are missing a massive chunk of the education bit.

Rastamouse motivated me to go and bang on a producer's door and this in turn created an opportunity. As a result I have seen broadcasters making real efforts, but we need to try even harder. Animals, robots, made-up species and shapes are involved in all kinds of brilliant, amazing, inventive and exciting story content but this worries me because I just have to make sure that the five-year-old me, the six-year-old me, the seven-year-old me could now watch a show and see one character that looks a little like me … whatever the show is ultimately about!

Growing up, having that would have meant so much.

Off-screen diversity is really easy. The talent is there – they are waiting to be invited in. I'll say it again: THE TALENT IS THERE! They have incredible stories to tell and share! Meet them for coffee! Employ them! Commission them! Let's stop talking about diversity at special events and put our money where our mouth is! Let's take some risks.

If we commission and make the right content, shining beacons of content that celebrate the real world, we can inspire and attract a whole new generation of talent who will prove that diversity is easy. Just open the door and we can do the rest!

DIVERSITY – ARE WE THERE YET?

ANGELA FERREIRA

—

The answer is that we are on our way. Hopefully we won't come across a great big hill and end up sliding backwards twice as fast as we are moving forwards.

Children's TV has always featured presenters and contributors who are diverse in terms of age, gender, race, accent, nationality, sexuality and disability. Drama and animation are both quite inclusive and the industry applauded the groundbreaking CBBC documentary *I am Leo*, which told the story of a transgender child. (See the 2015 Yearbook for the story about how that was made.) The women and girls who appear on children's television are presented as equal to men and boys – they climb, run and row, often breaking world records in the process. There's no gender bias there – females on kids' TV can take on any challenge and win fair and square.

Recent adult dramas have also featured more diverse casts and tackled tough themes, often involving young people. The primetime BBC 1 drama series *The A Word* is about a couple that struggles cope when their son is diagnosed with autism.

Undercover, which focuses on a black family and has many supporting black characters, features a teenager named Dan who is on the autistic spectrum. His lack of social awareness is crucial to the plot. And kids with Downs' syndrome have featured on every UK soap, going right back to *Crossroads* on ITV in 1983.

Of course we can always do more, and do it more boldly, but kids' TV is fairly healthy in terms of diversity. CBBC in particular seems very ambitious in choosing content that reflects the diverse lives of children across the UK and beyond. But in order to have truly diverse content we need a diverse workforce, and some groups, particularly BAME (black and minority ethnic) people, are underrepresented. All the major UK broadcasters have devised initiatives to address this and to stop the decline in the percentage of BAME people in the industry – in recent years there has been a drop of about 20% across the production workforce.

A report released in late 2015 by Directors UK was extremely damning about children's TV, noting that only 1.77% of all episodes in all genres was directed by a BAME director. The report found this "particularly alarming" as children's programmes are "a key entry point for the directing workforce and where directors get a first opportunity to develop skills that can be used in other genres." Indeed, many directors working as named documentary directors or on the main studio shows developed their core skills in children's TV and have gone on to work successfully and consistently, some at international level. The report concludes that "the role children's programmes have played in developing (BAME) talent appears to be at significant risk".

There is hope that the new Diamond* monitoring project from the Creative Diversity Network and the major broadcasters will provide clear statistics about on who makes TV and who is on TV and will comprehensively cover all aspects of diversity. We'll find out whether schemes like Extend, the BBC scheme aimed at attracting disabled candidates, or the Paralympic coverage at Channel 4 have succeeded in embedding staff into permanent media jobs. If not, we'll be able to ask why.

The Diamond monitoring project asks for perceived and actual information on gender, gender identity, ethnicity, age, sexual orientation and disability, but not on class. This is an area where "unconscious bias" is perhaps the most prevalent, and efforts to address it such as removing names, schools and universities from application forms should be welcomed.

Fully representing the diversity of the British population should be an integral consideration for every production, and the teams who make kids' content should reflect our country's diversity, too. Children want to see their real lives reflected on screen and they deserve honesty about the world around them. I love Katie Morag and her adventures on CBeebies and find her isolated community fascinating, but Morag might want to leave one day – and she shouldn't get a shock when she does. ◯

*Diversity Analysis Monitoring Data

THE VALUE OF VALUES IN THE WILD (NORTH) WEST

JON HANCOCK

Vegetarianism, Rolls Royce and the Mackintosh – all have been pioneered in the fine city of Manchester.

I'm fascinated by stories of how things came into being. It's why I love being a content producer – drawing together people with their various expertises, driving passionately towards an end goal, then pulling over to look back and admire the view together. I'm attracted by the sense of becoming a team, a *family* even … and I love how, when we're working with the right people, we are greater than the sum of our parts and have the capacity to create legacies.

I wonder: did the ironically (and hysterically) named Rev Cowherd think that his passion for meatless eating would rub off on his congregation and evolve into what it is today? Did Mr Rolls foresee that his Midland Hotel meeting with Mr Royce would result in a car brand synonymous with luxury? Did Thomas Hancock (no relation) ever dream that his masticated rubber, together with Charles Mackintosh's coats, would still be celebrated practically *every day* in these north-western parts where they were first manufactured?

These people all managed to collaborate with others, creating things that outlived themselves. I really admire them for that. And they all had seminal moments in Manchester – a place that's close to my heart.

As far as I'm concerned, the 2015 Global Liveability Survey had it right when it named Manchester the best British city to live in. There will be more devolution of power to Manchester over the coming years (we get our first elected Mayor in 2017) and the World Summit on Media for Children will be held in Salford at the end of next year – not to mention our world-class sport, arts and culture.

Despite the rain, I fell in love with Manchester when I moved here six years ago. It was a privilege to be one of the first BBC movers from London to the North West in 2010, producing the first series of *Mr Bloom's Nursery* from the BBC's old base in Oxford Road a whole year before MediaCityUK was opened.

So it is with an enormous amount of pride and excitement that I now step out from the BBC into the northern powerhouse to plant a flag in the Manchester sand (or should that be mud?), forming a new production company specializing in live action children's and family content: Three Arrows Media. The first of its kind in the North West – well, this century!

I do so with my friend – and now business partner – David Hallam. We initially connected because of a mutual friend and our shared Christian faith (more on that later), but we also joined forces because our skillsets complement one another. David has a proven track record of winning commissions across a wide variety of genres, target age groups and broadcasters all over the world, which dovetails with my (I'm chuffed to say) BAFTA award-winning production experience.

Parting from the BBC mothership – a place I am truly grateful and fiercely proud to have worked – has been challenging. One of the first pieces of work David and I did when we were considering a joint venture was to discuss and *define our values*: not just what type of content we wanted to create, but WHY we wanted to create it. What was important to us and what did we want to stand for? Something simply clicked – it just felt *right* – when we agreed on what our values were.

I have been inspired by the talks I've seen online by Simon Sinek. He has been described as an unshakable optimist (and he looks uncannily like Leonard from *The Big Bang Theory*), and I would heartily encourage you to watch one or two of his TEDTalks on YouTube. He talks about the importance of starting with WHY, in business as much as in any other area of life. A connection at this deep level can create bonds of trust, lasting relationships and incredible productivity and success.

> "All organizations start with WHY, but only the great ones keep their WHY clear year after year. Those who forget WHY they were founded show up to the race every day to outdo someone else instead of to outdo themselves. The pursuit, for those who lose sight of WHY they are running the race, is for the medal or to beat someone else."
> Simon Sinek, *Start with Why: How Great Leaders Inspire Everyone to Take Action*

As someone new to business ownership in the industry, I don't pretend to speak from a place of knowledge or experience. But I want to humbly encourage us all to establish our values (if we haven't already), and to question them; then to use them as a basis for connecting and creating with others. I believe this is the way we will most productively navigate through this new digital landscape, this new Wild West.

For Three Arrows, our values are "Creativity, Integrity, Excellence, Collaboration, Boldness and Fun." We know that we share these with many of you in our industry and therefore look forward to nurturing the working relationships we have and establishing new ones, serving other people's missions as well as our own.

So what's the story behind Three Arrows? In a lesser-known passage of the *Bible*, two guys – really good friends – have a decision to make about which direction to take. The decision is of national importance and requires them to communicate in code with one another.

Their plan is that one of them will fire three arrows into a field, and the other one will know, from where they have been aimed, where he should go. A small boy is sent to collect the arrows and carry them home.

The first reason this story jumped out at us is because the two guys, like us, are called David and Jonathan. But we also use the story to motivate us and root us in what we believe: that the children's media industry is of major importance. What goes into young minds has big implications. We want to create content that has meaning and value – that entertains and enriches – launching it out into the field, where we hope children will find it and take it home.

We would also love to think that our partnership could somehow outlive us. Our Manchester legacy may not reach the heights of vegetarianism, Rolls Royce or the Mackintosh, but nothing ventured, nothing gained! Life is short and can only be lived once, and so we step out with no regrets, for adventures unknown, trusting in the value of values.

> "People don't buy what you do, they buy why you do it. And what you do simply proves what you believe."
> Simon Sinek, *Start with Why: How Great Leaders Inspire Everyone to Take Action*

Twitter: @3ArrowsMedia
Website: www.threearrowsmedia.com

LITTLE BABY BUM

DEREK HOLDER

—

When my wife and I launched Little Baby Bum, we had fairly modest ambitions. We didn't for one minute think we'd be the number one educational channel in the world after just four-and-a-half years – or ever, for that matter. We set our sights much lower. We were complete animation novices when we started, and we aimed to get approximately 100,000 views per video per year. It was simple mathematics based on probable CPMs and the fact that pretty awful nursery rhyme videos were attracting ten million views or more. We figured that if we were to make better-quality videos and SEO them correctly we'd stand a chance of replicating those numbers.

Looking back I think it was our realistic, relatively modest targets that allowed us to breathe and not put pressure ourselves to achieve too much too quickly. We gave ourselves time to learn what we were doing, and we saw our mistakes as opportunities to learn – we didn't let them hold us back.

When we launched Little Baby Bum, my wife was a full time mum to our little girl (whose nickname was "Little Baby Bum" when she was just two weeks old) and I was working full time at a telecoms company. We built our YouTube channel in our evenings and weekends. Our output was slow. Very slow. There was a gap of four months between our first and second videos and we weren't massively pleased with the final results. But we did learn a lot from the process of making and uploading videos and from there we were able to develop and refine our project workflow. Over the following year we produced one video every six to eight weeks, which was all we could handle in our limited time. But we got a glimpse of what was possible and we realized just how big a YouTube channel could get. In order to bulk out our online presence we took our existing videos and created instrumental (or karaoke) versions of them, and made mini-compilations with around five or six videos in each. We also chose songs with variations in the lyrics – "Itsy Bitsy Spider" and "Incy Wincy Spider" featured the same video but different audio tracks, and we made both a zee and a zed version of "ABC".

After the first month our channel had 17,000 views. By month four this had gone up to approximately 400,000. I remember these numbers very well – we were excited because it proved our calculations had been correct. We knew that if we had 100 videos we'd be able to make a proper go of it. As time went by we reinvested our AdSense revenues into making more videos and uploading them more often. This in turn increased the revenues coming in, and so on. After two years of organic growth, we decided that we could go full time and put a hundred per cent of our energy into the channel. Our child would be starting nursery, too, which would really help. It was another six months before we were actually able to go full-time, due to work commitments, but from day one we started producing one video per week. We soon were able to increase this to two videos per week and have recently increased this again, to three.

My advice for anyone setting out on a similar journey is to make sure you create from the heart and don't make what I would call "cynical" content. Don't think about merchandising possibilities when you're creating children's programming. If you concentrate on creating a programme children will love, there's every possibility that you'll be able to move into licensing and merchandising, which is our next venture. In 2016, Little Baby Bum toys and books will be released in partnership with quality licensees and 2017 promises more toys and books as well as magazines, DVDs, clothes and so on. It's a truly remarkable time for Little Baby Bum and we're loving the ride. We adore receiving messages from parents who have seen how the videos help their children develop. What a lovely way to make a living – spreading joy to children all around the world while allowing their parents to have ten minutes peace, usually to have a shower or do some housework!

ANIMATION UK

OLI HYATT

—

"I'm only an elected official here,
I can't make decisions all by myself!"

First, ten points if you know the film that quote is from. Second, I'm sure you're wondering what I'm going on about, as usual – many of you have received a barrage of long, badly worded emails, requests for data and quotes and strange messages from Animation UK that must at times have seemed like an inner monologue on my various concerns about the animation industry.

I thank you all for humouring me while I taped ducks to hockey sticks, invited myself to your constituencies so I could throw myself at your MPs and persuaded you to ship delicate animation sets to the House of Lords. I apologize for cajoling you into parting with money for reports and speaking out in the press when you really shouldn't have, and the numerous other things I have asked you to do. Fortunately the mass-march of costumed characters on Parliament never happened.

I thank Blue-Zoo (Adam Shaw and Tom Box) for allowing me huge chunks of time to support Animation UK when I should have been growing our animation business. I'm sorry to those I've upset, offended, argued with, debated with and (in one case) stolen coats from in the name of Animation UK and children's TV. I'm also sorry that many of you didn't get the plaudits you deserved for your part in the campaign for tax credits – I feel embarrassed and humbled that I have seemingly become the poster boy (or silly mascot) for our joint enterprise. Anyway, I digress...

Those of you who are now ten points richer know that the quote at the start of this piece is from *The Nightmare Before Christmas*. "I'm only an elected official here, I can't make decisions all by myself!" It's a statement that, flipped on its head, unpicks the current issue with Animation UK. I'm *not* an elected official, and in the main I *have* been making decisions all by myself, albeit with much feedback from the industry. I've loved every minute of it, and I have, with your support, managed to get us a seat at the table. We now have a voice and, thanks in part to the tax credits, we still have an industry. I'm constantly thrilled and inspired by the flair and determination with which you run your businesses and the creativity of the work you produce.

But for some time I've felt that there is more work to do than I alone can cope with – more than any organization run on favours and passion can cope with. What we need now is a well-funded, well-run professional organization that can use our passion and creativity and the UK's unique reputation and position in the world market to move our industry to the next level.

Since I first announced this move from "club" to "industry body" at the CMC event in March, I've received near-unanimous support from all of you, and many of you have signed up and fed into what could become a mandate. I feel hugely positive that we can achieve great things. We have commitment from over 50 companies and enough funds to turn this dream into a reality.

There's still a lot of work to do to get this right – there needs to be much due diligence and a formal process for setting up the membership structure. We need to find the right person to drive this forward in the long term and to set up the board or committee. We need to agree goals and set out a shared vision for what achievement will look like.

In the short term, we will need to address issues around training – the government is moving money away from old training structures and into apprenticeships, which we don't currently have in our industry. There are other pressing political issues, with the Charter renewal rumbling on, that will effect us all one way or another over the next ten years, and new issues that have arisen from the tax credits and changing EIS rules. We need a report that properly calculates the value of our skills – I have spoken to the BFI about jointly funding this, and the conversation needs to be picked up. In the short term this would be a more viable way of tracking our industry than the government's SIC and SIC codes, which can only be changed every few years.

But as well as pressing problems, there are pressing political opportunities. For instance, George Stanley is to become our first well-informed DCMS policy advisor. He wants to immerse himself in our industry over the summer, so please welcome him to your studios.

The aim is to get a comprehensive understanding of how the animation industry in the UK works so this can be best represented to ministers – how are projects planned, scoped, funded, produced and sold; what are the usual routes into the industry and how is it taught; what are the crossovers with other industries like film and VG; who are the big and small players in the UK?

Many of you are looking at cultural funding to reignite our proud heritage in short films and, in turn, bring through the next generation of film makers. Lots of you want to see us out en masse at events, presenting a united, friendly face and letting the world know about our great industry. This will mean becoming a trade partner, and we will look into doing that as soon as possible so that we can access the support others currently enjoy, such as TAP grants.

As an industry, we have been hanging onto the coattails of other organizations for too long. For the very small minority that think this is just another organization and that we have enough of those already (The People's Front of Judea, The Judea People's Front), ask yourselves this: who is really putting us first? Who is prioritizing our needs? Who really helped us when our industry was slipping away? No one. Everyone turned us away, and some even tried to stop us. We helped *ourselves*, and I believe that as we move forwards, this is the strongest and most powerful thing we can continue to do.

The results speak for themselves. While no real numbers have been gathered (because we don't technically exist), anecdotal evidence tells us we have doubled in scale in the UK and have grown by 600% in London. While TV commissioning remains challenging, I believe there are

currently more opportunities for animators and visualization artist than ever before in the UK.

That doesn't mean we won't continue to work with others – we are the beating heart of so many of the screen industries, and we will work with PACT, CMF, CMC, BFI, Screen Association, IPA, UKTI, UKIE and many more. But more power and money will give us more influence. We'll be able to shift the agenda to include animation and be the voice of authority on matters that affect us.

However, we need to be realistic. A portion of the first year's fees will be spent on getting this initiative up and running, and it will take time. There is a chance we could work more closely with another body to save on admin costs, but we would need to make sure that this wouldn't dilute our message.

I fully intend to continue to engage with the organization on a long-term basis, and in many ways I expect my workload for Animation UK to increase in the short term. I will stand to become an elected official in whatever form the organization takes, so if I've annoyed you or stolen items of clothing from you, feel free to join just to vote me out! I very much hope this is the end of the beginning and that we'll be able to move forward in a positive way! ◯

THE IMPORTANCE OF BEING DIFFERENT

JOSHUA DAVIDSON

Hello! I'm the Night Zookeeper. Welcome to my zoo. Well, it's not exactly *my* zoo – it belongs to all the children who have created a magical animal to come and live here. We have all manner of strange beasts, from spying giraffes that can turn invisible, to a purple octocow that can make any flavor of milk that you can imagine! I wonder – could *you* invent a unique animal to come and live in my zoo?

Removes hat

Hello again everyone. I'm sorry about that. I slipped into school assembly mode for a minute. I'm Joshua Davidson, CEO of Night Zookeeper, a children's company that has spent the last four years asking children to invent their own unique animals. It has been an incredible experience – a journey into the imaginations of hundreds of thousands of children from across the world.

I set up Night Zookeeper because I believe there is a major problem with digital games today. Too many of them simply give children a limited range of preset options, which means that handing a child an iPad is like handing them a keyboard that can only play preloaded songs. This is not a great recipe for creativity, and it certainly doesn't make full use of the incredible technology available to us today.

Night Zookeeper, by contrast, allows children's imaginations room to breathe, so that they can create and invent as wildly as they would on a piece of paper. The question "Could *you* invent a unique animal to come and live in my zoo?" invites children to express themselves.

Sadly, some children struggle to fully embrace this opportunity. A common misunderstanding is that these children just don't have the capacity to be creative. However, scientifically speaking this simply isn't true. Creativity is a skill that can be mastered. But some children – and some adults, too – avoid creative thinking because they fear being different, and because they're afraid of failing. Society allows these fears to fester and we see them manifest in children on a daily basis. It breaks my heart.

I set up Night Zookeeper with my co-founder Paul Hutson, a former primary school teacher who has travelled the world delivering lectures on the importance of teaching creativity in the classroom. In his role as head of literacy at the highest paying fee school in Abu Dhabi, he recognized the limitations of teaching today and he saw the potential of Night Zookeeper to change things. Together with a team of designers and developers, we started to build nightzookeeper.com, a drawing

and writing platform for children of all ages that actively teaches creativity.

We have failed a lot along the way. Our Night Zookeeper apps were loved but never made any money. Our first incarnation of the nightzookeeper.com website was too "educational" to be a true consumer proposition, and it arrived at a time when website subscriptions were fast going out of fashion with parents. We learned from our failures, however, and we embraced Night Zookeeper's destiny to become educational software.

This year we have sold Night Zookeeper software licenses to schools across the world, launched a virtual reality app so that children can see their drawings come to life in a virtual world, and published a physical storybook. However, we are far from finished. We are still failing and learning all the time.

The temptation to be the same as everyone else is incredibly powerful and deeply ingrained in our society. At

Night Zookeeper we are doing everything we can to try to challenge this and to reduce the impact of the desire for conformity in schools. But the entire children's industry needs to work together to affect real change. Therefore I want to end with a rallying cry.

In 2016, let's set a better example to children – let's try to be as different from each other as possible. Let's reject the safe path and take risks and push boundaries. Let's try listening to our own hearts and embracing the unquantifiable rather than just studying the successes of others. Let's learn as much as possible about the business of inspiring the next generation. Most importantly, let's not stigmatize those who try something new and fail. Instead, let's celebrate them for their bravery and embrace what they've learned.

Children aren't born with self-doubt – it is learned behaviour. As an industry that serves up children's stories – the ultimate vehicle for education – we can teach kids to believe in their own ideas again, to take risks, and to have fun with their intelligence. That is what our story is about. What will yours be? ◌

THE STORY OF
LOST MY NAME

DAVID CADJI-NEWBY

——

Once upon a time (in 2012), a little girl was given a personalized book for her birthday. It wasn't a very good book. In fact, it was a rather bad book. But still, it made her father think. Made him think, *Hmmmm. There's an opportunity here.*

Asi (that's the dad) got in touch with a couple of friends. One, Tal, was a digital producer. The other was David, a comedy writer. The plan that they hatched was to make a personalized book – a better one than had ever been made before. A personalized book that didn't just copy and paste a child's name into a pre-existing story. No, one that used a child's name to form the narrative of the story, so that no two names made the same book. A perfect combination of storytelling and technology.

The concept of the book was that a child loses their name and goes on an adventure to find it. Each letter of their name relates to a story, and helps them get their name back. So if, for example, the child's name is Andrew, they'd go on an adventure to meet an Aardvark, a Narwhal, a Dragon, a Robot, an Elephant and a Wizard. Each character gives Andrew the first letter of their name. A, N, D, R, E, W – hey presto, he's found his name.

Now, this wasn't very easy because, annoyingly, there are twenty-six letters in the alphabet. Not only that, but lots of names have more than one of the same letter in them. And every single letter needed its own story. And, of course, every story needed illustrating.

We worked on the book in our spare time. Evenings. Weekends. Any time we could find. Which meant we had to have understanding families and plenty of discipline. We found Pedro, our amazing Portuguese illustrator. And slowly, *Lost My Name* started to take shape. We made a prototype book, for Andrew, with stories and illustrations, and showed it to people. The people told us that it was good and that they'd absolutely, definitely, no question buy one.

Then came the real challenges. Finding a print house that could print the books on demand. Building the website and the back end. Doing the marketing. Fulfilling orders. We launched in April 2013 and sold a few books. Then Christmas came, and orders came in thick and fast. We weren't ready. We really, really, really weren't. It was madness. We went from 40 orders a month to 40 a day. A hundred a day! Scaling was a colossal task. We had a bestseller on our hands and we'd never planned for it. We weren't complaining, no, but we were running around like the proverbial blue you-know-what.

Next came *Dragons' Den*, where we got a record-breaking deal from Piers Linney. More investment came in and we grew. We're "full-stack", which means that we do more or less everything in-house (apart from the actual printing). We write and illustrate the books. We write the software for the site. We do all our own customer service, marketing and PR. It takes a lot of people.

Our original mission was to make a million bedtimes more magical with our book. We used to say it as a joke, only half-believing it was possible. A million? It's a huge number, unimaginable. But in 2015, we did it. We hit a million (and became the UK's bestselling children's picture book). And we know, from the thousands and thousands of emails that we get from our customers, that our book really does seem magical to the children. We know that we're doing a good thing. And that makes us happy, too.

It's hard. Of course it is. We have employees and we need to pay them and keep them cheerful. We have investment, so now we have targets. We need to launch new books (we've already launched our second title, *The Incredible Intergalactic Journey Home*, based on a child's address). We need to get into new markets (we've already translated into ten languages). We need to keep innovating, and scaling, and surprising and delighting children around the world. But as missions go, creating magical bedtimes is a rather splendid one, we think.

CBBC OFFICIAL CHART SHOW

STEVE WYNNE

—

It's fair to say the "Hit Parade" runs through my blood – I religiously taped the pop charts every Sunday from the age of nine, presented a Top 40 show on Hospital Radio Clatterbridge, and went on to produce ITV's CD:UK. So when CBBC approached Pretzel to pitch for a new music chart show, it was the most exciting thing anyone could have asked me to do.

For the best part of a year, there had been high-level discussions between CBBC and Radio 1 about how to bring the *Official Chart Show* to TV. Keen to strike the perfect tone, CBBC commissioner Hugh Lawton and controller Cheryl Taylor asked us to put together a pilot – on a budget that made even me, king of the discounted biscuit, weep into my instant coffee. What I didn't reckon on was the new generation of talent who think nothing of being able to shoot, edit, write, direct and make the tea – and can do them all brilliantly.

Pretzel has a scheme that brings in first-timers and nurtures their skills. Our VT directors Michael J. Ferns and Fergus Thom hadn't made a frame of TV in their lives, but they came back from self-shooting and directing 300 pupils at a school for a Taylor Swift lip-dub having edited a roughcut on their laptops on the train. Our production manager Millie Lloyd, who hadn't seen a call sheet until she started with us, gave us a masterclass in how to get anyone to do anything by being polite, all while choreographing, researching and location managing the show. Oh, and

she also presents our vlog. And Myke Dunn stepped up from listening to Blink 182 in his recording studio to become our sound engineer (and associate producer). Not only was he able to create and produce tracks and record on location, he also stepped into Nick Grimshaw's studio and mixed the live show.

There's a severe drought of music shows on TV, and almost nothing for our audience. We were determined to create something unique and fresh that would play to viewers who consume content in a totally different way from audiences reared on 30 minutes of *Top Of The Pops* each Thursday. Rather than just counting down the chart, we wanted to make the show a true appointment-to-view – something that would be talked about in the playground on Monday mornings.

Now you can see performances anytime, anywhere – from wobbly gig footage to multimillion-dollar promo videos – so we wanted to create exclusive content that lived on, away from the show, that could be consumed and shared whenever and wherever.

We created some standout moments that have had tens of thousands of views – and make the chart alive and relevant for 2016.

The idea was always to broadcast the show from the Radio 1 studios, home of the DJs that inspired me to get into the industry. To say I was beside myself about this is an understatement. Radio 1 has come a long way since the days of my heroes Bruno Brookes and Mark Goodier. It now has a visualization team led by the ever-willing Joe Harland. As the instigator of hours of video content, from the Live Lounge to Greg James' infamous David Attenborough and Adele moment, Joe was the reason we were able to set foot on the eighth floor of New Broadcasting House.

All we had to do was take a radio show and turn it into a 30-minute live extravaganza for telly – every week. It quickly became apparent that with a team of four, who were already filming and producing the VTs, we might be a little stretched. So we pulled in a few favours, took a few shortcuts and, with our presenter Cel Spellman, we delivered our pilot and waited to hear the result.

Cut to early 2015 when CBBC ordered an initial 26 episodes, then extended it to 66 (!) and we realized this was truly going to be a labour of love.

We had two short days of rehearsal before embarking on the live run, so we had a fair bit to work out. It was a proper learning curve for us all.

The vision gallery at Radio 1 only seats two, so I moonlight as studio director, vision mixer and VT op.

ORIGINAL VIDEO

Our first TX was almost a total write-off. Our VTs had a codec that the system hated; I had to key open one of the talkback keys with one hand and use the other for vision mixing or running VTs; our guest was half an hour late; and we didn't have enough mics.

At 18:21, nine minutes before going on air, we were informed that our bars and tone were both illegal, and then the entire disc-based VT system crashed. I wanted to have a little cry into my BBC instant coffee.

Somehow, we rebooted, told TX to take it or leave it, and bounced onto air with the *CBBC Official Chart Show*, bang on time.

Even though I'd worked on hours of live TV at SM:TV and at the Disney Channel, I had forgotten the sheer adrenaline

and pace of a live show. There is nothing like it.

We've filmed in schools, homes and shopping malls up and down the country with flashmobs, acapellas, lip-dubs and cameos (you'll have to watch to find out who appears).

Our booker Luis Pulido got Jason Derulo to interview himself, we've fed Fifth Harmony cold scotch eggs, given piggyback rides through Radio 1's offices and asked everyone to sing their name for as long as possible.

Frankly, I'm amazed we've got away with it, because the show shouldn't work. It's produced by a team who have never worked in TV before, on a couple of laptops and loaded onto a PC with a memory stick.

But it does work. That's testament to the real change that has happened in the 20 years since I started working in TV.

300 TO 3 TO 1

SIWAN JOBBINS

—

300 to 3 to 1. No, these aren't the odds on Eddie the Eagle attempting a ski jump at the 2018 Winter Olympics, but the number of projects at each stage of CBBC & BBC Worldwide's animation scheme, ANIM8.

Back in October 2015, CBBC, in partnership with BBC Worldwide, announced the launch of the channel's first animation pilot scheme, ANIM8: an open call offering UK creatives the chance to pitch for funded development. Both partners had been looking for an opportunity to work together to develop a comedy series with genuine global appeal and when an opportunity arose to bid for an internal BBC fund, we seized it.

What is ANIM8?

As Henrietta Hurford-Jones, director of children's, BBC Worldwide, said: "BBC Worldwide's mission is to take the best of British creativity to the rest of the world. Our ambition is to find creatives and concepts to mirror the success of titles like *Sarah & Duck* and *Hey Duggee*, but this time we're on the look out for character driven, fast-paced comedy which will appeal to older kids." This new, exciting partnership offered UK innovators the opportunity to work alongside CBBC and CBBC Worldwide's creative teams to develop their projects for the domestic and International market.

What were we looking for?

Compelling character-driven content, which was funny, energetic, unpredictable,

upbeat, and which had a unique take on contemporary life. The scheme was looking to push visual boundaries and was open to all animation styles and techniques, including mixed media. As Sarah Muller, creative director, scripted, animation and co-productions for BBC Children's noted, "Launching the ANIM8 pilot scheme was an ambition realized for CBBC. It is an exciting time and a key step in our continued objective of nurturing home-grown animation talent and producing original, innovative animated series that resonate with the CBBC audience."

Who was eligible to participate?

We welcomed content from our fantastic production companies and studios, but we were aware that many of the UK's talented creatives are not tied to them, so we were keen to see projects from individuals such as writers, animators, storyboard artists and animators. We're delighted to say that they applied in droves.

What was the process?

The submissions process closed on 22 January 2016. Entries were assessed by the ANIM8 team, which included Cheryl

Taylor, controller of CBBC, Sarah Muller, CBBC's creative director, scripted, animation and co-productions, Henrietta Hurford-Jones, director of children's, BBC Worldwide and Nathan Waddington, head of children's, scripted at BBC Worldwide. Projects were judged against criteria such as originality, international appeal, premise, world and characters, and – first and foremost – comedic appeal. Following this rigorous process, our 300 entries became eight. These diverse and engaging properties were given a small development budget and following a short development period were re-submitted and judged again. Our eight then became three.

Who are the final three?

We are delighted that our final three include several new names as well as established individuals, reflecting our aspiration to tap into the wealth of talented people who work within the UK's creative sector.

Mystery Soup is a surreal comedy about three plucky 13-year-old girls investigating their weird new boarding school and the bizarre goings on there. Created by writer Victoria Manifold and director Hannah Jacobs, Mystery Soup follows

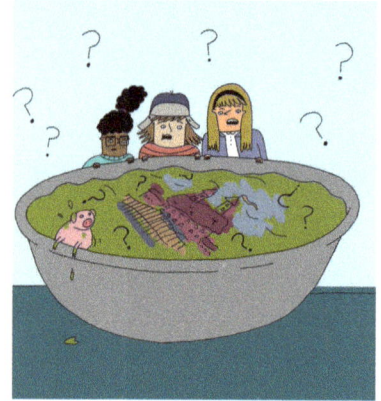

Mystery Soup

the adventures of Hen, Olive and B as they find themselves plunged into mystery at a handsome school for dedicated boys and girls.

Hannah Jacobs is an award-winning director and animator from London. Past clients include *Vogue*, *The Washington Post* and Harvard University. Victoria Manifold is a fiction writer from County Durham. She has been published by *The White Review*, *The tNY Press* and *Squawkback*, among others.

Peeled Prawn and Shaved Sheep is an exciting new series following the adventures of a genius sheep and his shell-less friend. With the help of his Prawn Powered Super Shell Suit, Prawn and Sheep battle Mr Big and his gang of super villains whilst juggling work, home and finding love with the mysterious Lucia Langostina. With a distinctive comic-book

Peeled Prawn and Shaved Sheep

Poles Apart

visual style and clever snappy dialogue, it's the summer blockbuster superhero series with a twist. *Peeled Prawn and Shaved Sheep* is created by Vince James, Karina Stanford-Smith, Simon Godfrey and Kaine Patel.

Karina Stanford-Smith is an experienced animation producer and has produced such shows as *Tickety Toc* and *Florries Dragons*. Vincent James has directed animated shows for CBBC, ITV and Dreamworks TV.

Simon Godfrey's involvement in TV has spanned production, development, design and promotion for clients such as Amazon Prime and The Jim Henson Company. Kaine Patel owns Snipple Animation, which services such productions as *Dora the Explorer* and *Bunnicular*.

Anarchic and Antarctic, *Poles Apart* is an animated, action-packed character comedy, following the adventures of Ryder, a haphazard elf banished from Santa's grotto to live in the South Pole with Santa's brother, Sandy Claus. Ryder's job is to deal with the massive, never-ending Naughty List,

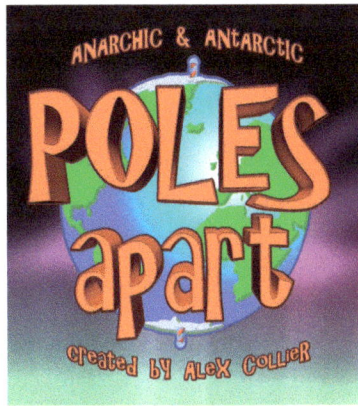

and encounter naughty kids the world over! Ryder, Sandy and techno elf Irwin must all work together, despite being completely different to one another, truly making them all Poles Apart!

Poles Apart is created by Alex Collier, a *Viz* comic cartoonist who has recently written on *Mr Bean: The Animated Series*, and even more recently, the *Danger Mouse Comic*.

What next?

For the final stage, following some additional development time, the three projects (now complete with scripts, visuals and a bible) will be pitched to our team. The lucky winner will work alongside the CBBC and BBC Worldwide creative teams to develop their project through to a pilot. To paraphrase those scions of UK pop, the Spice Girls (with our tongues firmly in our cheeks), three will become one. Watch this space…

Good luck, guys!

THE RECIPE FOR DIGITAL-FIRST SUCCESS

JULIET TZABAR

—

Back in 1994, I was working in one of my first jobs in media. I was a temporary PA to Heather Holden-Brown, then a cookery book publisher at BBC Worldwide. I would come into work and find a pile of dictation tapes on my desk and I would spend my days playing the tapes back, typing out letters to the BBC's leading cookery talent – chefs and television producers. I remember starting numerous letters with the words "Dear Baz," referring to Peter Bazalgette, now a TV veteran. In those days he was producing *Ready Steady Cook* and soon after became credited as the man who invented the celebrity chef. It was clear then that Peter worked in television, while Heather, my boss, worked in book publishing. Media production was platform first. You worked in television, radio or print and you created content for that platform, using established production methodologies, developed over years.

Today, media production exists in a very different landscape. Digital delivery demands that we must adopt a platform-neutral mindset, developing and creating content that can be delivered in multiple formats. Legacy media, such as television, radio and print, are no longer the primary platforms of consumption. Digital media has muscled in, be it via online, social media or app delivery, and content is now increasingly created according to a digital first methodology, with the digital debut of content becoming more and more commonplace.

Returning to 1994, my temporary contract in the world of publishing came to an end and I returned to my freelance work as an art director for television. It was another six years before my interest in media convergence would be piqued by the internet and I would adopt a digital-first mindset for my own career, finding work as a digital producer, funnily enough on another Bazalgette production, *Big Brother*.

I now run Plug-in Media, a digital-first production company that doesn't define itself by the platform it delivers to. We are not a TV production company, an app developer, a games company or an animation studio, although we make all of those things – we are simply a production company making content in a new(ish) digital landscape. However, indulge me now as I return to that formative experience in cookery book publishing (I've always thought of it as my alternative career) and consider some of the analogies that cookery offers us, as I share Plug-in Media's recipe for what a digital-first development and production methodology involves.

1. Assemble the best ingredients

While platforms proliferate, the appetite for great content remains consistent and the best products emerge from the best-quality ingredients. Think of the early stages of digital content development as an opportunity to browse the best market produce! The tomatoes are piled high; artisanal goat cheeses are stacked on boards; and sea bream are laid on ice, fresh from the nets that morning. You don't know what dish you're going to make yet – but you're happy to immerse yourself in the sights, sounds and smells of the market atmosphere and take your time touching, sniffing and tasting the produce.

Similarly, before we decide what the end product of a digital-first development will be, we immerse ourselves in the core ingredients of story, setting and character. What we're aiming for is a deeply conceived DNA that we know will ensure a product's authenticity on whichever platform it ends up. Our mantra has become "You can't retrofit story and character" – you need to make sure they're built in from the start.

In the case of our own IP, *Tee and Mo,* our core ingredients were simple: a new mum, her three-year-old son, their relationship and their jungle home. We worked really hard to develop these characters and their world before we knew what product we were pitching. We knew that if they were drawn with depth and authenticity they would survive the limitations of whichever platform they ended up on.

2. Consider your consumer

You may have gathered the best ingredients, but there's another decision to make before you decide on which dish to make: who are you cooking for? Some chefs are so certain that their balance of seasoning is perfect that they refuse to provide salt and pepper on their restaurant tables, but this stance takes the confidence of the auteur, and in an environment without limitless funds, some regard for needs of the consumer is advisable. This applies to the creation of children's content in particular, because of the diversity of the audience. Just as you'd create a different dish

for a vegetarian than you would for someone with a nut allergy, so your output will be different depending on whether it's created for pre-schoolers, 6–10 year olds, or teens – and we all know that kids can be the pickiest of eaters!

These demographic boundaries are not new to media production, but viewing them with a digital-first mindset will lead to a further consideration that will profoundly impact your production process: access. A platform-neutral mindset accepts that your audience will have access to a number of different media devices: a TV, a computer, a tablet, a console, a mobile phone, an MP3 player etc. You will need to understand the nuances of your demographic to appreciate how access to these different platforms might be impacted by cognitive development, social class and gender.

3. Preparing your dishes

Beyond considering which combination of devices and screens your audience has access to, in the post-appointment-to-view world you also need to think about the mindset they bring with them to those screens. You may have decided at the market that the verdant watercress, fresh duck eggs, earthy mushrooms and springy sourdough were the very best produce on offer, but is this a dish for a weekend breakfast, a quick lunch or a starter for a celebratory dinner party?

In creating *Tee and Mo* we conceived of a brand featuring a parent and child that directly reflects the nuances of that relationship back to the audience. Our first *Tee and Mo* dishes were web games that parents and children could play *together*. We intentionally created something that was about co-play and shared screen time for a sit-forward moment in a parent and child's day. With this in place, we realized we also needed a lean-back piece of content. We developed the "Who Did the Footprints?" story for CBeebies Storytime and the brand's short-form, animated lullaby "Go to Sleep" to answer that need. Same ingredients, different dishes, different cooking methods.

And you need to respect different cooking methods. One of the most common assumptions about digital-first production methodologies is that if you make something once, it will fit everywhere. This is the mindset of those who are desperately trying to justify the cost of producing multiple transmedia products by assuming that the cross-pollination of assets will lead to efficiencies in the longer term. It rarely works like that, especially when you're combining HD broadcast assets with the plethora of different technical platforms. Making both dishes simultaneously may result in efficiencies of time and money, but it could also force you into making decisions you weren't ready to make and, in the worse case scenario, you might have to pop out to the shops to buy more eggs to start the cake again!

4. Taste and season, easy on the salt

The hard work is nearly over. You've made your dish and it's almost ready to serve. Hopefully the quality of your original ingredients shines through and you haven't been tempted to add Worcester Sauce, a carrot, some bacon and a few chocolate chips in an attempt to give it more flavour. The aim is to work quickly and confidently, delivering what software product developers define as a Minimum Viable Product (MVP).

If you're heading for the Masterchef final, your MVP won't be the final version of your dish but the first one you put in front of a customer (perhaps a forgiving husband, niece or neighbour).

The first taste is an important one, and in this brave new world of digital-first production, it's OK to get it (a little bit) wrong. Ideally your willing taster will enjoy the dish, but they might have a couple of suggestions to make: a bit less chilli next time, an extra teaspoon of sugar wouldn't go amiss. These suggestions are going to help you to improve on what you've made before you place it in front of the judges. Your tester will be flattered that you listened to them and will be eagerly anticipating the next course.

Returning to our IP, *Tee and Mo*, our ten web games on the CBeebies website delivered the first public outing of our monkey duo (although they'd also been tested on a friendly neighbour or two beforehand). In less time than it takes many kids' IPs to emerge with a bible and a pilot, we had a finished product in front of an audience and were using that product to shape the brand going forward. We had quantitative data that told us how many people had played the games and we had qualitative data that told us what they liked about them and what we should change. We had also managed to create a self-fulfilling appetite for more content, which has since led us to create the app, e-story, animated shorts and the album of songs, all of which are available today. Furthermore, we've been able to use this data to justify investment in a 50x7-min TV series.

5. Sit back and enjoy

I'd like to finish my first cookery book with a summary revealing how this process has led Plug-in Media to become a three-Michelin-Star restaurant (er, sorry, I mean production company). The truth is, we're still working on it. There isn't yet a three-month waiting list for tables but we do serve many happy customers every day. We know that they're enjoying the dishes we create. We're continuing to refine those dishes and we're also inventing new ones. We've been investing in our kitchen equipment (a talented and diversely skilled twenty-first century production team) and we're always striving to select the best-quality ingredients, allowing them the space to be the stars of the dishes.

We've also had some good reviews – the respect of our peers has come in the form of BAFTA and Prix Jeunesse nominations for *Tee and Mo* (does that count as one Michelin Star?). We're trying not be swayed by fashionable ingredients or fads for the latest cooking techniques (is VR the new sous-vide?). We hope that these slow-food principles will lead to long-term commercial success, but for now the proof remains in the half-eaten transmedia pudding!

WILL A BETTER UNDERSTANDING OF CHILDREN MAKE ALL THE DIFFERENCE?

LUCY GILL

—

I spend the majority of my time working with people developing children's media, particularly apps both big and small, and they always want to know if there's a secret recipe for success. Of course there are never any guarantees, but there are several factors that, if ignored, are highly likely to lead to failure.

For the purposes of this article, I'll take it for granted that you've got a great basic concept and feature set for your app, wonderful graphics, an experienced team and a strong marketing plan. Surely you're sorted? Sadly not. There is one set of stakeholders that is often overlooked or consulted only as an afterthought – children.

Whether you're developing an app for children or adults, anyone who has been in this game a while will tell you that user experience (UX) is important. But for children's media, the issues around UX are vastly more complex than for products aimed at adults.

The fun factor

If you want children to engage with an app, it really does need to be fun. Are you sure you know what kids find funny? You can add playful graphics and silly animations and hope for the best, but I've tested enough apps to know you really need to check your app with children to be sure of success. Often I find it's not the overt, laugh-out-loud features that make a children's app a hit – at least not beyond the first five minutes. It's the subtle, playful ways the app engages children and the features that help them gain confidence or motivate them to have another go.

Let's take an app I know

well as an example: the new Happy Studio app from McDonalds, which I've been involved with since the concept phase. You'll find plenty of "fun" features – children find it hilarious when they tickle Happy and get him to stick out his tongue – but, according to our testing, the part that really gets the most attention is the Inventor game. Children are clearly motivated to succeed, often through much trial and error. Subtleties like the app's ability to make failing fun (the car breaks apart as it falls into the ravine, for example) make all the difference.

Learning and development

I'm always keen to find ways to incorporate learning and development into media for children, even if it isn't the core purpose of the product. After all, there is a reason gamification is taking over the world – what better way to learn than by having fun? But if you don't understand children, it is almost impossible to pitch the educational dimension at the right level. Children change so fast, particularly in their early years, and a firm grounding in the skills children are typically developing at your target age

is crucial to success. There are huge cross-cultural challenges to consider too, particularly for international apps. For an app to be useful in developing a skill, it needs to hit that sweet spot between challenging and totally impossible.

UX for children

I still often see classic mistakes when I'm reviewing apps for the Good App Guide – preschooler apps requiring the child to read, for example – but often the UX challenges are much subtler. We know children like to learn and discover things for themselves rather than having to sit

through first-play tutorials, and yet if the gameplay isn't intuitive they will quickly brand an app "stupid" and never play it again. When producing an app for children, it's so important to remember that it needs to be as simple as possible both for them to find or initiate play and to understand how to play. The gamplay should be challenging, not in the UX. User testing is the only way to really be sure you've got this right. Toca Boca is a brand that really puts the emphasis on UX, with very good results.

Avoid addictive features

One critical factor for success, as far as I'm concerned, is making sure that an app isn't genuinely addictive. Of course we want our products to be successful, but it's important not to go too far. Excessive screen time is a real and growing problem for children, and as players in this industry it's vital that we don't intentionally make this worse. By all means make apps fun and engaging, but try to build in natural "end" points that give children

a chance to switch off.

When you take all the factors above into account, it's clear that you have to involve children in the development process to ensure that your app will be successful. What's more, testing apps with children can make teams much more innovative – they'll have the chance to trial new ideas with the app's intended audience rather than just playing it safe. This really doesn't have to be wildly expensive, nor should it delay your schedules – I've turned around results within a few hours to extraordinarily tight budgets. My tips are:

• **Upskill your team**
Ensure your team has a good basic understanding of children. Hold seminars and encourage team members to share their knowledge of different ages and stages of

development. Plan a fun family day – a great way to get children involved in the development process.

• **Get children involved early**
Don't wait until you've got a finished prototype – start testing at the concept or storyboarding stage. Look for competitors or similar apps to learn from, too.

• **Test little and often**
Don't try to answer every question during one round of user testing. Plan regular, focused testing stages and get someone independent to facilitate the sessions and analyze the results.

• **Include a children's ambassador**
Assign someone to attend key meetings as the voice of the children. Involving children in your development process really can make all the difference.

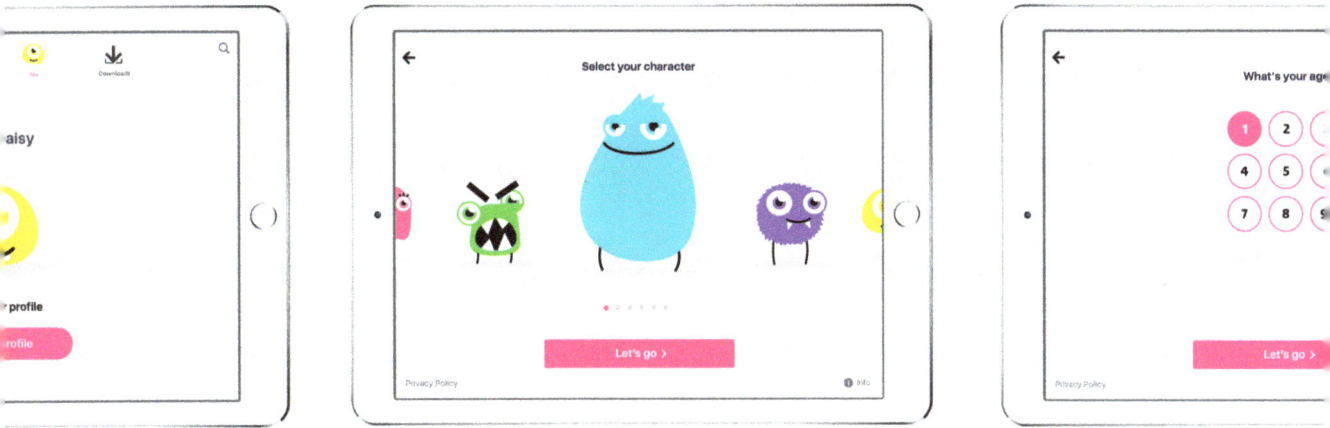

KID'S IPLAYER

CLAIRE STOCKS

It's 1977. *Star Wars* has just hit the silver screen.

I'm alone in my bedroom. The family black-and-white portable TV is mine for once, for a few hours. It doesn't feel particularly "portable" as I lug it up the stairs. It's tuned – albeit in a grainy, flickering snowstorm – to *The New Adventures of Batman*. I sharpen the white noise back into a picture, poking the makeshift coat-hanger aerial with my foot. I feel a million dollars. For the first time in my life, I have total control of what's "on the box". There are three channels to choose from, showing a couple of hours of children's TV per day.

Today, our kids have an unbelievable amount of choice – there are 32 dedicated children's channels in the UK. The BBC alone shows 26 hours a day across CBBC and CBeebies, and most of those hours are made in the UK. Kids also have unbelievable control. On the right devices, those shows can be paused, watched again, saved for later.

Kids *expect* choice and control. Parents too, are actively looking for services that offer them, especially services they can trust and configure. This has led to the proliferation in the last decade of child-specific services, including, in the last 18 months, Video On Demand (VOD) services, and that's why we launched BBC iPlayer Kids in April 2016.

2016 was a significant year for media consumption among kids in the UK. The definitive Childwise report, which tracks the behaviour of children aged 5–16, stated that – for the first time – the numbers of hours children spent online

89

outstripped hours spent watching TV. On average, children spent three hours online and only 2.1 hours watching TV (though this varies hugely by age).

Does that show the demise of TV – or could it point to its future?

It's 1987. Rick Astley has just hit the pop charts.

Little does he know how kids of the future will react as he rick-rolls his way into their lives through the internet.

The growth of video recorders was meant to kill off cinema (as well as the radio star). But as we moved to digitally served, on-demand TV and film viewing in the home, cinema enjoyed a renaissance and some video-rental chains went bust. Changing consumption sparked by digital revolution isn't always a case of "either/or". Often, it's a case of "and".

It's 1997. Teletubbies has just hit TV screens. Eh-oh.

The BBC has also launched its website. Within a few years, the buzzword will be "convergence" – the idea is that there will be one device to rule them all.

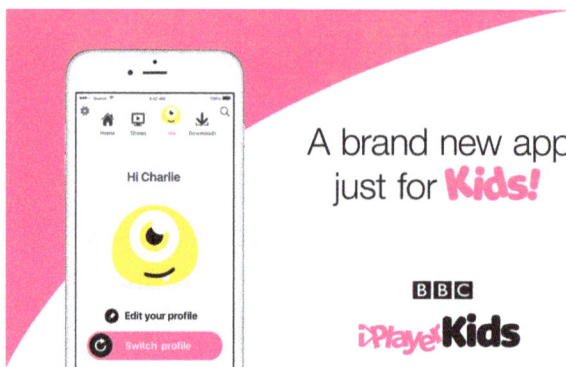

A brand new app just for Kids!

BBC iPlayer Kids

"Divergence" might have been more apt. We now think about audiences' differing experiences via laptops, phones, tablets, e-readers, wearables, game consoles, virtual reality headsets … the list will only get longer. And it still includes the big screen in the corner of the room!

The forecasters forgot one thing: human nature, which drives us to want the best thing for the specific activity we are performing. This is why we have myriad different types of chair in our houses and why washer/dryers never took off!

So I view the data from Childwise as three hours *plus* 2.1 hours. It's a different equation – it's "and", not "or".

Even Childwise concede the delineation between "TV" and "online video" is a grey area – they told us they leave the question of which is which up to kids own interpretation. It's safe to say that much of

kids' time online includes watching on-demand TV via touchscreen devices. It also includes YouTube – which is now the number one reason kids aged 7–16 go online. And a third of children who use Youtube are watching TV titles. Which of us can categorically define what we watch as "online video" or "TV"?

There is no easy answer.

Our own panel data shows that around 35–40% of 0–12 year olds watch TV online. They also watch video clips, play music and games, use social media and do homework, depending on the age of the child. So the lines are massively blurring between TV and online. We're not even sure what TV means anymore. Traditionally it meant the content you watched *and* the screen you watched it on. Now it can mean both, or either, or neither.

And while the overall volume of TV viewing on TV sets is declining, one thing we do know is that the televisual content we make is still very much in demand. Our children's content reaches over 40% of

0–12 year olds in the UK every week. But the way our content is being consumed is changing, and that's why we're changing too.

It's 2007. BBC iPlayer has just hit the web.

And in less than a decade, the service has fundamentally changed the viewing habits of all BBC audiences – especially kids. Available on more than 10,000 devices and packed with iPlayer exclusives as well as linear broadcasting, the service is still evolving in line with the demands and expectations of our audience. For example, iPlayer consumption is responsible for 45% of CBBC show *The Dumping Ground*'s seven-day ratings – note that's just the seven days immediately after broadcast. It's our responsibility to ensure that kids are served with the content they want, when they want it, where they want it.

But where do they want it? TV sets are still the preferred screens for viewing. Childwise data shows that 62% of kids prefer to watch TV on TV. But the proportion that *prefer* to watch TV on alternative devices is growing – it's now one in three, with tablets especially popular. When asked which device they "could not live without", the majority of 5–16s cited their phone, followed by tablets (17%), TV (16%) then games consoles (14%).

While on-demand viewing of children's content is rocketing, 63% of our audience are still viewing our content live. For some shows, like *Newsround*, that number leaps to 92%. And while TV is still the screen of choice for live content, when it comes to on-demand, we know that the majority

Future iPlayer Kids features

We've added the ability to resume a part-watched episode where you left off and given kids easier-to-reach recommendations at the end of an episode.

Next we're looking at episodes autoplaying one after another – but we want to find out more from the parents and kids who use the app to help shape that feature.

One of the things we're really glad we built in for launch is the ability to download content – many kids are instantly excited about being able to take their favourite shows with them, whether they're going on holiday or a long journey or even if they just want to take the tablet to that corner of the house where the Wi-Fi signal's a bit flaky.

Downloads can be kept for up to 30 days after broadcast and there is no limit to the volume of shows kids can download, only the space on the device (the app itself is around 25mb).

We also wanted to provide accessibility options as we take this very seriously when making products for kids, so there is the option to view signed or audio-described content.

What next? We have a few ideas, but this app is all about fulfilling our audience's need for control, so we'll let them answer that question.

of iPlayer viewing is done via mobiles and tablets – 53% of requests were via a tablet and mobile and 28% of requests were via a TV. So at every turn, the picture is more complex than a simple shift away from TV. It's about a proliferation of choice and control.

Which is why we launched BBC iPlayer Kids. In the last three years, requests in BBC iPlayer for children's content has tripled. In 2015, there were just shy of three billion programme requests via iPlayer. A third of those were for children's content. On-demand contributions for CBBC and CBeebies content are the highest of all BBC channels. Around a fifth of all viewing of CBBC TV content is now via iPlayer, whereas the average across all BBC channels is just 3%.

You'll see individual children's episodes remaining high in iPlayer charts for months; we are now scheduling our CBBC TV channel to ensure popular shows appear in iPlayer for long periods. Our peers at Swedish public service broadcaster SVT grew use of their VOD mobile and tablet app threefold by a simple change to the navigation which put users' last-watched shows front and centre on the

homepage. A recent survey by Sky found kids watch their favourite episodes more than 50 times a year.

But although kids want control and choice, we know kids they also relish shared family viewing. They often the ones asking parents to put down *their* devices to spend time doing traditional real-world activities, and it's encouraging to see that reading books and playing outside are still popular activities (one in three kids still read every day). This is why our app is only a small part of the way we're responding to the changing landscape. It's also why we don't just rely on feeds and algorithms in BBC iPlayer Kids – we also actively curate our content. A skilled team of experts tailors it both in terms of time of day and age. During the week, our audience likes shorter clips in the morning and longer programming in the evening. For children aged 1–4, we show only CBeebies content; for children aged 5–7, we show a mixture of age-appropriate content from both CBeebies and CBBC; and children aged 8-9+ are shown just CBBC content.

It's 2017. We've learnt even more about our audience, through BBC iPlayer Kids.

Ok, I've not got a time machine. Yet. But we'll be back at CMC in 2017 to tell you how our audience is using the app and how we've responded to our viewers' demands.

We're starting to add select short-form episodes alongside our channel titles. In our first week in app stores, one of the standout pieces of content was a beautiful short film about being a child in China, from *Newsround*. And in the future we want iPlayer Kids to become a home for the best content from across the BBC – we know kids get huge value from right across our portfolio. The most-watched BBC linear TV for 6–12 year olds are shows like *Eastenders*, *Dr Who*, *The Great British Bake Off*, *Casualty* and *BBC News*. So we're looking at how we can curate popular shows that are right for kids of different ages, on-demand – what they want, where they want it, when they want it.

For nine-year-old me in 1977, that would have meant delight in an endless feast of *The Six Million Dollar Man* – but I doubt, sadly, the more edgy *Starsky & Hutch*. Some things never change.

"NEVER WORK WITH CHILDREN OR ANIMALS" – W.C. FIELDS

RAY MAGUIRE

—

I ignored W. C. Fields' advice during my brief few years in theatre (I was on the technical side, not a luvvie) and during my games career (kids played a significant part in making PlayStation a household name). So what are the challenges of working in an environment that is centred around children, especially when you're a new high-tech start up?

Working in a huge, well-known company has many benefits:

- Infrastructure – there are experts in every facet of the business at your fingertips
- Funding – pre-defined budgets allow you to concentrate on the job in hand
- Brand recognition – doors open for you with little or no resistance
- Networking – especially valuable when working in different territories.

Start-ups are a completely different kettle of fish. No longer can you rely on well-funded research and development and decent marketing budgets. On the plus side, although you take all the risks, you get to make the decisions that will shape your journey going forward without being distracted by endless reporting that never seems to add value to the outcome. For me, the decision to take the plunge into the world of start-ups was based on the fundamental belief that my co-founder Andy and I could add value to the education system by introducing new technology in the form of a Cloud-based video platform.

Education is the third

largest spend in the UK, at almost £90 Billion, but teacher costs account for the vast majority of this, at around 76%. The remaining 24% covers everything else. The budget for new tech in schools is in single digits. From a route-to-market point of view, the majority of schools make their own decisions on the budget priorities. There is a small but growing shared-services provision, as the number of Multi-Academy Trusts has increased in recent years, but the majority of decisions are still made in-house. A head teacher's job can be a rewarding but lonely one, as they have to balance the demands of the staff as well as the pupils and parents. It's therefore vital that any new tech service offers a solution to all the stakeholders involved in decision-making processes. In a commercial environment, if you can demonstrate that the implementation of new tech will lead to a return on investment, then funding can be raised and paid back over time. Unfortunately for schools, budgets are fixed and any investment is at the detriment of spend in another areas.

But what about the teachers themselves? The brutal truth is that the education sector is struggling to attract new teachers. More teachers are leaving than entering the profession and inevitably the gulf is widening. The reasons for this are multi-faceted, ranging from pay and conditions to stress and lack of support.

How can technology help busy teachers? Anything that saves time and reduces stress has to be a good thing. Couple that with a platform that lets pupils express themselves in a medium that inspires them and hopefully you'll have a product that ticks most of the boxes. It makes perfect sense that exam boards are introducing video assessment. Qualitative and quantitative outcomes will be measured without the stress of a traditional exam scenario.

The use of tech in schools is very varied. The majority use tech to great effect, but we still come across schools with cupboards full of unused tablets, bought with very best of intentions but without establishing the implementation and pedagogy first. The majority of pupils have grown up with access to the internet and numerous devices, and they are able adapt almost seamlessly to new software solutions. But less tech-savvy teachers need more support.

Schools have had to adapt to an "always on" world and the initial reaction was to ban mobile devices in schools rather then implement strategies to use the new technologies whilst preventing disruption. Safeguarding has always been a priority for schools and the rise of social media continues to pose problems. Teachers are increasingly becoming attacked through social media by pupils' parents, with or without justification. Ever evolving technology demands an evolving technology strategy to produce the best results for the school and defend against attack and disruption.

Used creatively, technology can bring subjects to life and make learning more accessible. There's nothing better than walking into an outstanding school and seeing first hand how a good teacher can nurture the talent of the pupils in their care. If our platform can help them achieve even better results, then I'll consider the journey from big business to start-up a major achievement. ◎

SECRET LIFE OF BOYS

ONE CLICK, ONE LAUGH: HOW WE MADE OUR INTERACTIVE COMEDY

TREVOR KLEIN

—

Secret Life of Boys was commissioned as an interactive comedy before anyone quite knew exactly what that meant. The subsequent figuring-it-out took the better part of two years until, finally, everything just "clicked".

Writer/creator Anthony Q. Farrell (*The American Office*, *The Thundermans*) first wrote and pitched *Secret Life of Boys* as a regular sitcom. The story begins with 11-year-old Ginger Boxwell flying from Australia to the UK to spend the summer with four cousins she's never met before, understandably nervous about how she'll manage in a foreign country with a new family. What she doesn't realize is that Matt (17), Robbie (13), Ethan (12) and Chris (7) are just as nervous about it as she is. The boys soon discover that Ginger is hiding something. And it's BIG. The game is afoot and they work tirelessly to uncover Ginger's secret, all the while trying to protect their own.

At the time, CBBC's Cheryl Taylor didn't have any more room for regular sitcoms, but she did need some digital content, so in a heartbeat the affectionately acronymed SLoB became an "interactive comedy", though at the time nobody quite knew what that meant.

What we ended up with was a new kind of comedy drama for the touchscreen generation. SLoB is made up of

25 x 5' interactive episodes and 50 x 1' unlockable secrets, all combined in a playful hub which launched online last November. The programme was then repackaged and broadcast as 5 x 22' traditional episodes for CBBC and ABC3 Australia.

How it works

The critical question that needed to be answered was, could we legitimately claim that adding interactivity would enhance the sitcom genre? If the answer was no, why do it? If the answer was yes, then how?

"One click, one laugh" was our mantra, and our interacting players were rewarded with unexpected punchlines, ridiculous replays of the action, surreal adventures and surprising new perspectives.

As you watch the interactive episodes on your tablet, phone or desktop you'll see playful buttons pop into view. Nobody's forced to click and the episode continues without pause for those who choose not to. But for those who do interact (and it's almost everybody), clicking unlocks hidden gags.

As an additional layer, players can also collect "secrets". Within each interactive episode, there are two glowing objects – they might be a phone, a knitted hat, a discarded football shirt, anything. When the eagle-eyed player clicks on them, they unlock secrets to watch later. These secrets are delivered intimately to camera, revealing hidden insights into a character and the wider story. (Spoiler alert: alpha-brother Matt is a secret knitter and confident joker Robbie is afraid of the dark.)

If you manage to collect enough secrets, you get to unlock Ginger's Big Secret – a huge story surprise that rewards you for your dedication. Throughout the series, both characters and audience are united in trying to discover the real reason behind Ginger's move to the UK, with speculation running wild in the CBBC comments.

How we made it

Our executive producer Steven Andrew set the tone clearly from the start: the digital delivery was not a bolt-on or afterthought – it was integral, and the heart of the commission. This meant we needed to create a whole new development, production, post and delivery process that blended the best of traditional TV and traditional software development.

Zodiak Multiplatform (hat tips to Ben Freeman and Joe Dickinson) had spent a lot of time evaluating different interactive video platforms. They wanted to find something that would work equally well across mobile, tablet and desktop, and that was powerful enough to be customized to create linking videos. The clear winner was WIREWAX who, at the time, were the only company who'd found a way to circumvent Apple's technical restrictions to bring interactive video to the iPhone browser.

With WIREWAX we had our technical platform, and we already had our characters and storyline, so the last thing to crack was our format.

We were keenly aware that 22 minutes of linear video is a very, very tried-and-tested format for comedy drama, so it was no small responsibility to break it apart. We took great care from the start to avoid making our interactive show a poor cousin to a traditional sitcom, instead working to invent a new, just-as-satisfying digital-first format that enhances the form.

We started with a basic insight: children like to have more of what they enjoy. We tried to empower them to get just that each time they clicked ("I liked that joke – I would like more jokes similar to that joke please"). We also knew that our audience are fascinated by secrets – having them, sharing them, discovering them – and realized that giving our characters personal secrets would enhance our comedy, world and story. To figure out the detail, we spent a lot of

Image credit: Helen Sloan

time brainstorming and sharing examples of digital "stuff" that we found funny: websites, apps, games and videos.

We ran frequent test shoots – we filmed scenes in offices around Zodiak Kids HQ, drafting in runners (and each other) as stand-in actors. This embarrassing footage was then turned interactive and we could quickly see whether or not our ideas were working. As we grew more confident, so did our test shoots. Producer/director Beryl Richards organized one in her home, and children from a local theatre group gave much more convincing performances than we had. Indeed, one of the test actors impressed everyone so much that he went on to play youngest brother Chris in the series.

When writing the show, Anthony created a new scripting grammar that included the extra

interactive material and patiently wrote and rewrote many, many drafts as we all learnt together. We had input and feedback throughout the process from both broadcast and digital commissioners at CBBC and ABC3 Australia, as well as from our audience. We went into schools to test our work-in-progress episodes with mixed groups of 6–12s. Not only did we get their ideas and feedback on our UX, design and digital creative process, but also on our jokes. This was a new experience for Anthony – there aren't many sitcoms that go through a rigorous user-testing process(!), and we have the feedback to thank for the amount of physical comedy in our show.

Creatively, we arrived at some very fixed ideas about how the interactivity should work: it's not a "choose your own adventure" branching narrative, but a "dive into the adventure" where players get more of the gags they like. Everyone gets the same crafted, satisfying story.

There's no download

or app required – everything streams to your device from your browser. There's no forced interaction. It's all optional and positively reinforced (with either more jokes or more secrets). There's no punishment for not interacting or gates that require interaction before you can move on.

We had a fairly ambitious amount to film each day (about 7–8 minutes), so these guiding principles stood us in a good stead when we started shooting on location in Northern Ireland. While our crew was used to normal location drama, everyone adapted quickly to the quirks of our production. For instance, many of our shots needed to be held for an unnaturally long time, to allow for an on-screen button to be added later in WIREWAX. Art department and costume had to be briefed on continuity – what happens if a character makes a mess during an interactive scene, which not all players will see, but that same scene continues on afterwards?

We had a similarly ambitious amount to edit. With 111(!) different video deliverables we worked closely with Platform Post Production to set up a process that would enable us to get everything edited, delivered and complied between Zodiak Kids Studios, WIREWAX, CBBC and ABC3. One giant colour-coded spreadsheet later and we had a breakdown of what was happening where for each day over four months. I'm told that when it was printed out at CBBC HQ it took up 12 A3 pages. (There were a lot of spreadsheets in this production.)

Logistically, none of this could have worked at all without the full support and trust of our excellent commissioners at CBBC and ABC3 Australia (both broadcast and interactive). There was a lot of heavy lifting to be done internally at both broadcasters to let us deliver to their platforms, and a seemingly endless stream of videos, designs and builds to feed back on. We were lucky to have them.

The reception from our audience, both online and on TV, was heartening. We had huge engagement with our interactive episodes – much higher than expected – and streams of positive comments from passionate fans on the CBBC and ABC3 websites. The repackaged linear TV omnibus episodes were equally successful, beating their slot average on CBBC every week (on several occasions by twice as much) and frequently charting on iPlayer.

We know that children are still watching a lot of television, but we also know that they're increasingly doing so on smaller, more personal, smarter devices. What we've proved with *Secret Life of Boys* is that there is a space for new TV formats that make the most of what these devices can offer – not replacing linear TV, but complementing it, and empowering children to choose whether or not they want to interact. And it turns out, when given the option, most do. ◯

www.bbc.co.uk/cbbc/games/secret-life-of-boys-game

(Best enjoyed on a modern tablet with speedy wifi.)

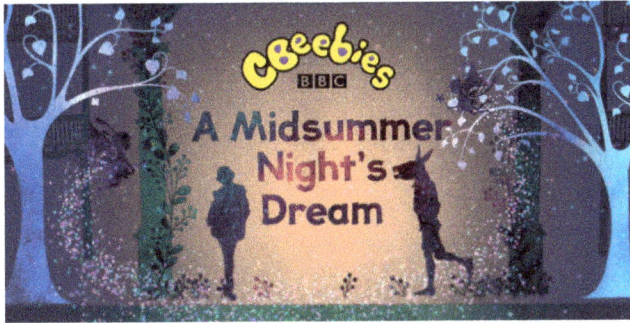

SHAKESPEARE AND PRESCHOOL – WHO SAID THAT THEY DON'T GO TOGETHER?

ANGELA YOUNG

When the BBC started excitedly discussing how to celebrate Shakespeare's 400th anniversary, there was an assumption that CBeebies couldn't be involved. Kay Benbow, controller of CBeebies, took this as a challenge and started thinking about just how CBeebies could be part of the celebrations. Theatre adaptations of classic stories are very much part of the CBeebies landscape – past productions have included *A Christmas Carol*, *Peter Pan* and *Alice in Wonderland*. The partnership with Northern Ballet has expanded the audience's appreciation for storytelling in different forms, and stories are completely at the heart of all the channel content.

Shakespeare was a brilliant storyteller – so why couldn't we tell one of his stories in a CBeebies way?

Alison Stewart, head of CBeebies production, felt that there was one obvious story to tell – full of fairies, magic and with a name every pre-schooler would love. *A Midsummer Night's Dream* would be the perfect introduction to Shakespeare. Which little one wouldn't laugh at Bottom's name? How much *more* would they laugh if he was played by Justin Fletcher? The programme was taken forward by the CBeebies development team and executive producer Tony Reed before I started working on the production in October 2015.

So where to start?

The approach

What would make this Shakespeare production different, unique to CBeebies and memorable to the pre-school audience? It had to be the approach. We would have to help the audience understand what was happening onstage and what the dialogue meant, and give reminders at useful moments of what was happening in the story. With Cook and Line (established characters from CBeebies' *Swashbuckle*) to ask the questions, we were half way there – but who would answer them? There was only one person for the job – Shakespeare himself!

Going through the cast of CBeebies talent, one person sprang to mind to play Shakespeare: Steven Kynman, aka Robert the Robot in *Justin's House*. He had all the CBeebies experience but, out of silver paint, he wouldn't have pre-existing audience character expectations. With online material to introduce Shakespeare, we could expand the impact of the programme with facts and figures to intrigue young minds as this historical figure was introduced.

The story

How many of you remember *A Midsummer Night's Dream* from school? What do you remember of the story? From the outset it was important to find the key elements to drive the story through, simplifying the plot while retaining as many crucial moments as possible so that children would remember them in the future. I set about creating a grid with the original action in each act and scene, then pared it down to essential story elements to form the first story running order.

At times it felt like I was back sitting my Highers (yes, I'm Scottish), working my way through various editions of the play including those with education notes. I wanted to make sure I wasn't missing anything that Shakespeare had intended through changes in language, rhythm, characterization and setting. A trip to see *Henry V* at the Barbican renewed my enthusiasm for Shakespeare, and also ignited a crucial set idea.

Finally, when I thought I had really grasped the play, I set about putting together a programme proposal for Ali and Kay. I recently re-read the proposal and I was delighted to see that the finished programme is very much true to the original idea and structure. The proposal combined Shakespeare, Cook and Line's backstage action with the onstage production, showing how integrated the concept had to be. The proposal included quotes from the original text to demonstrate that we would use Shakespeare's dialogue wherever possible, and also demonstrated how our backstage team could help explain what a play is and what the various theatrical elements were. Additionally it briefed the music elements that would be key to keeping the audience engaged.

Partnerships

A first impression of Shakespeare has to be right. We knew the programme would influence so many children and their parents and carers – so pronunciation, rhythm and interaction had to be correct. Developing a relationship with the RSC gave us somewhere to find advice and support as well as the right people to work with the team.

We held rehearsals at the RSC's new building, The Other Place, and RSC practitioner Nia Lynn was performance director, providing a huge amount of support and inspiration to the CBeebies talent who felt challenged by taking on Shakespeare. But with Athenians, Young Athenians, Mechanicals, Fairies and Young Fairies, 25 actors were required, and the regular CBeebies cast had to be expanded. Advice from the RSC head of casting was crucial in getting the right balance across the roles.

Location

What kind of theatre did Shakespeare write his plays for, and what would make this production different for our audience? The search was countrywide. We didn't just need to find the perfect theatre – we needed to find somewhere to introduce live theatre to children who wouldn't usually have that experience. The immediacy of the performance was vital – a proscenium arch theatre felt too distant. A trip to Liverpool and the Everyman Theatre with its thrust stage solved the "where". It also sparked lots more ideas. We were recommended a lighting designer and a set designer who had worked extensively at the Everyman. Neither had any television experience but they were willing to learn – they came to see other productions and were ready to ask

Barrie Bignold took on the challenge, creating a song that combined Elizabethan motifs with a modern approach and the original text. This approach worked so well that it was used for Puck's song too. However Bottom's song had slightly more complex and less suitable lyrics, so we decided to use this as a moment of fun for the audience – a song where they could laugh along with Bottom, Cook and Line. Three original songs, sung by our Shakespeare, highlighted important action moments – setting up the play, changing scenes and helping to recap and resolve the story in a simple and effective way. Finally, the Bergomask dance combined Elizabethan dance with text that little ones around the country are now singing. These songs, combined with music beds written to picture during the quick turnaround post-production period, kept the audience engaged without distracting from the play.

questions. A costume design lecturer from LIPA brought a great, young team on board, giving local talent a chance to develop as well as diversifying our crew base.

Music

Every Shakespeare play ends with a song and dance but music is also integral to the overall performance. *A Midsummer Night's Dream* has three songs within its action – "Puck's Introduction", "The Fairy Lullaby" and "Bottom's Song". Could these songs work for our audience?

BBC Learning working with British Libraries had established a great opportunity for the CBeebies version of "The Fairy Lullaby" to be distributed during National Shakespeare Week, a month prior to our transmission. The one stipulation was that the original Shakespeare text had to be used. Composer

Text

The decision to keep as much original language as possible was definitely one of the biggest challenges. I worked closely with writer Clare Duffy on the abridgement, identifying sections that would work easily for the audience as prose, phrases which would need explanation, words which would need to be replaced with alternatives, and importantly finding the soliloquies that could stay at the heart of the play and hold the attention of the impressionable audience. Initial cautiousness about the concept and word "love" disappeared after discussing the play with groups of children and hearing their versions of the story. The first scenes featuring the Mechanicals worked, with some editing for length, without changing the text – and during rehearsals it became clear that the delivery and action in these sections would make them comprehensible without the need for explanation, which would have interrupted the flow.

It really was a balancing act between the play and the backstage action, but finding ways to make things memorable was fun too. "Athenians" is an awkward word, but "Athinynnians" is a great comedy word – Cook and Line's misunderstanding of quite a few words definitely kept the tone age appropriate and light hearted. The audience's engagement with the text is one of the greatest joys – it doesn't put them off. Instead they are intrigued and spellbound by the rhythm and delivery.

The wider team

Engaging the right team was key for the production – from the production management team that kept everything on track, to the technical team who rose to every challenge. The Everyman Theatre was perfect for the performance but was definitely a challenging TV recording space. With a single camera recording onstage while rehearsals went on offstage, every minute of the theatre and actors' time was taken up with multi-camera recording in the lead up to the live performances. Ian

Russell, TV director, kept on top of all the action and managed to ensure every single moment was captured with ISO recordings, including valuable audience shots to show the rapt attention of those in the theatre.

Of course there are too many people to mention, and so many elements that can't be described here – colour coding the young Athenian couples, the theatre's fantastic flying and trap facilities, working in a sustainable friendly theatre, filming interactive content, creating on-brand story versions for the CBeebies Storytime App and for CBeebies Radio, the trials of finding the right people to engage with our aims for the roles of Titania and Oberon, the great team atmosphere and smiling faces in the theatre all week…

But the main thing that I have taken away is that being brave and completely believing in something is so important. It really has been one of the best TV experiences I have had, and has resulted in amazing audience feedback. So I'll leave you with just one comment:

> "My youngest daughter (four next week) has watched *A Midsummer Night's Dream* about 15 times since it was on last weekend. This morning she had a friend over – also four – and they were taking it in turns to be King Oberon and Queen Titania. It's an absolute triumph – thank you so much! It's so good even I enjoy it (life-long Shakespeare-phobe!)."

JACKANORY

FRANK COTTRELL BOYCE

When I said I was going to the *Jackanory* birthday party, my friends howled their jealousy and swooned their nostalgia.

Lynda Buckley Archer said, "School often made me anxious. Snuggling up with Marmite on toast and *Jackanory* made me feel safe and happy." Nicola Davies said just hearing the theme tune made was enough to make her purr.

Of course, *Jackanory* wasn't always cosy. The unease I felt when listening to Charlotte Sometimes or the first Greene Knowe book put me right off my Marmite. Finding Miss Slighcarp in the slot I associated with that magical woollen muffler of a voice – Bernard Cribbins – was like finding a cluster of scorpions in my lunchbox. As for Tom Baker's crazed, intense reading of *The Iron Giant* … I still shudder now.

Loving a book on Jackanory meant I would hunt the original down, and its sequels, and other works by the same writer. But promoting and directing our reading was the least of its good effects. Far, far more important was that *Jackanory* made reading a shared experience. We often talk about reading as though it is a solitary, isolating activity. But for most of history, and certainly in my experience, stories have been things we share - around the fire, at the bedside, on the "story mat" at the end of the day in primary school and definitely on *Jackanory*.

Joolze Tudor remembers children charging around the playground yelling, "Neverrr. More!" after hearing Bernard Cribbins' hilarious rendition of Joan Aiken's *Arabel's Raven*. Phil Earle said that Rik Mayall's rendition of *George's Marvellous Medicine* seemed to burst out of the television. Next day at school, everyone was talking about it. "None of us could believe what we'd just seen," he told me. "It broke

every rule." Phil called it his first watercooler moment – like watching *Doctor Who* or *Game of Thrones*. I felt very much the same about Kenneth Williams reading *The Land of Green Ginger*. Joan Aiken and Helen Cresswell were the Russell T. Davies and Steven Moffat of *Jackanory*.

Jackanory helped create a shared culture for us – something that was not being shoved down our throats by giant brands or merchandising – hence all the swoons of nostalgia and these vivid memories. I would never have known *The House That Sailed Away*, for instance, or *Agaton Saxe* or *The Minnow on the Say*, without *Jackanory*. I hope it will be remembered for actively commissioning some truly wonderful work – I think I'm right in saying that *Mortimer the Raven* was made especially for *Jackanory*. And then there's the sublime Lizzie Dripping, who stepped into the world on *Jackanory Playhouse*. And of course the artwork. I'm pretty sure my first encounter with Quentin Blake was on *Jackanory* and that I learnt to appreciate the different voices of illustrators from watching the show.

I learnt so much from

Jackanory, and I'm not the only one. Brian Minchin, the producer of *Doctor Who*, wrote me a long, lyrical email about how that Tom Baker rendition of *The Iron Giant* had influenced him. "Looking at it now," he said, "what grips me is the utter belief that production had in the importance of the story it was telling. There are no layers of irony or nods and winks. This is a full-on and committed attempt to bring Ted Hughes to life on a tiny budget but with complete conviction … I'm only realizing it now, but it must have affected me, because that ingeniously created world and that commitment is something I'm trying to recreate now every day at work!"

That's a great legacy, but I think there was something more profound going on too. One of the unconsidered marvels of human complexity is our ability to recognize voices. When I switch on the *Today* programme halfway through an item, I often know who's speaking, even if it's someone who has been out of the public ear for years and who didn't mean that much to me anyway. This morning for instance it was – of all people – Norman Lamont. It never ceases to amaze and

delight me that I can recognize not just words and their meaning but the actual identity of the speaker. Even if they're nothing but an ex-chancellor of the exchequer.

How much more amazing and delightful to have these voices in my memory bank: Bernard Cribbins, Kenneth Williams, Joanna Lumley, Bernard Holley and Liz Crowther. And – someone whose voice I haven't heard since then but who I imitate when I read his stories, whose cadences are part of that intimate storytelling moment between me and my children – John Grant, who read *Littlenose the Hunter*.

Nostalgia is often regarded as a trivial emotion. But the complex magic of these voices pulls us back to a moment when our minds were fresh. They bless the present with the beauty of our past. They bring back to us the openhearted enthusiasm and willingness to listen that we had as children. The rhythms and cadences we heard while cuddled up with the Marmite continue to reverberate in our work and in our play.

Jackanory laid down in my heart as well as my mind a fund of stories that I can draw on now, not just for writing

or reading, but for when I'm troubled or bored or feeling lost.

Another person who reacted to my question about *Jackanory* was Michael Rosen, who said he had been booked to appear on it but the show was cancelled.

I was recently at a fundraising event for the Reader Organisation, which believes in the power of reading aloud. Its volunteers read big, ambitious books, not just in schools, but in prisons, in drug rehab centres, in hospitals, to people who struggle. One of the prison reading groups did *Henry V*. Afterwards, one of the prisoners who had attended the readings said something that went straight to the heart of how *Jackanory* affected me. This man was in for violent crimes, and the story of how Prince Hal rejected his old friends and began again really struck a chord with him. He said that listening to someone else read – knowing he was not going to be asked for any "input" or "insight" – was "the first time I had ever felt alert without feeling stressed", the only time he'd felt fully switched on without the threat of violence. That's what human voices can do.

Thank you *Jackanory*. Come back soon. ◯

LET'S START ACTING LIKE KIDS AND HAVE A GROWN UP CONVERSATION

ALICE WEBB

Across the globe, it is in equal measure the most exciting and the scariest time to be a child – a mix of emotions that all of us working in children's media can empathise with, as we are working through a time of unprecedented change, taking place at an unprecedented rate, within a constantly fluctuating media landscape. Audience behaviours now seem to shift on an almost weekly basis, and the sheer scope and quantity of content flooding the marketplace is impossible to stay on top of.

Of course, the rate of change varies greatly around the world, and children in different countries have different experiences. However, it's fair to expect the trends that many of us are seeing to spread around the globe in due course.

The media industry has always embraced change and hasn't been afraid to restructure itself over the past few decades, but it does seem that this time we are experiencing the most audience-led revolution so far. A fundamental shift in the traditional relationship between content producer and audience has totally changed expectations of what the media sector is there to do and what it is able to achieve.

We are no longer simply broadcasting to our audience; we are in a conversation with them.

In the children's media sector we have reacted to this change more quickly and, I think, more effectively than any other area of the media, but the journey is far from over.

Over the past year, we at BBC Children's have started to try and do things differently with this in mind – we recognize that a rapidly changing world is not something to fear, but is in fact hugely liberating. Through a new project, which has the working title "iPlay", we are looking at how to engage and interact with our audiences on a more personal level than ever before. The iPlayer Kids app that was launched in April of this year is an important step towards this.

Some have been quick to claim

that more choice somehow reduces the importance of BBC content for young people, but we believe the exact opposite to be true – that our responsibility to these audiences is greater than ever before. Never has our role as a producer of world-class content, crucial resources and laughter been more important.

The Reithian ideals, "Inform, educate and entertain", feel as fresh in today's digital world as they did in the world of the wireless all those years ago. I think you can now add "inspire" and "enable" to that list of ideals as well, as digital gives us the opportunity to create platforms and methods for like-minded kids to come together in safe spaces.

It is in everybody's interest that our sector remains as relevant as possible to the lives of young people across the globe, whether we achieve that by working together differently, creating content differently, legislating differently or ensuring freedom and safety for young audiences in ways we have never thought of before. That's why I chose to support the bid for the Children's Global Media Summit 2017 in Manchester, and to accept the role of chair when the bid was successful.

The summit is an opportunity for us to have a conversation defined by impacts and opportunities rather than genres and platforms. The aim is to assemble the best thinking from content producers, policymakers and platform providers together in the same place, with the needs and wants of young audiences around the world as the main topic of discussion.

Crucially, this is not a BBC event – it

is much bigger than that. This is a global gathering, led by the World Summit on Media for Children Foundation, which has been helping to facilitate joined-up conversations across our sector since 1995. The BBC is lending its name and backing to the 2017 summit as we recognize what a crucial milestone it could be in shaping our business over the coming years.

At the first Foundation event over 20 years ago, a TV charter was proposed and adopted, setting out principles for how global broadcasters should manage their relationship with young audiences. Subsequent summits have updated and extended this work, and we will continue to do so in 2017. We aim to create a digital-first charter with agreed protocols for operating as an industry in a digital space.

I would love to welcome as many of you as possible to join us, both in Manchester next December and in the conversation going forward as we shape and develop the summit itself and create legacy projects that will live beyond it. To make sure we continue to serve our audiences and stay as relevant and meaningful as possible, we need a grown-up conversation about what it will mean to operate in children's media in the coming decade. I hope the Children's Global Media Summit can be the start of that conversation, and if you want to be there so your voice is heard, or you would like your company's CEO to be among the leaders present, do get involved. You can find updates at www.cgms17.com.

CONTRIBUTORS

Rebecca Atkinson

Rebecca Atkinson is a freelance journalist and creative disability consultant for kids' industries. She has experience in TV production, print journalism, online content and scriptwriting. Rebecca has a specialist knowledge and interest in the media representation of disability. Rebecca worked for 11 years at the BBC as an assistant producer on a range of factual and children's programmes and later produced and wrote for soap, teen and music websites for BBC Online. Rebecca has contributed articles and comment for publications including *The Guardian*, *Vogue* and *Marie Claire* and has written three screenplays for Film 4 and a play for Soho Theatre, London. In 2015, Rebecca co-founded the online #toylikeme campaign calling for positive disability representation in toys. She is available for creative consultation for toy brands, TV production companies and advertisers looking to include positive representations of disability. Previous clients include Playmobil, Orchard Toys and Lucie London.

Gregory Boardman

A co-founder and director at The Rastamouse Company, Greg is a creative producer, musician and writer who worked with the show's creators to develop *Rastamouse* into a multi-award-winning television series. In addition to his extensive experience developing scripts and new projects for television, Greg has also played an integral role expanding the Rastamouse experience into music, radio, live programming and The Rocksteady Reggae School education project. He is currently producing a brand-new live-action series that will launch in 2017 and is also researching the role of music in education at the Institute of Education in London.

Nathan Bryon

Nathan Bryon is a 24-year-old (soon to be 25-year-old) actor, writer and Afro enthusiast. He has written for CBeebies, *Rastamouse* and *Swashbuckle* and is currently working on a new live-action children's show as well as starring in hit ITV comedy *Benidorm* as Joey Ellis.

David Cadji-Newby

David used to work in the big and rather scary world of advertising, writing ads, and then the surprisingly cut-throat world of TV comedy, writing sketches and sitcoms. He is a founder of *Lost My Name* and finds that writing books for children is altogether more pleasant and rewarding.

Alex Chien

Alex Chien is a consultant specializing in brand and creative management, based in Beijing. Her clients include Disney China, Shanghai Media Group, CCTV Animation, Beijing Design Week, the Swire Group and the Ullens Centre for Contemporary Arts. Before setting up her own consultancy, she was head of brand/general manager/VP of creative and content with Nickelodeon from 2004–2012, posted in Shanghai, Singapore, London and Beijing. Prior to that, she worked as executive producer and producer/director at Disney and MTV in Asia. alexchienn@yahoo.com

Dr Barbie Clarke

Barbie is the founder of children's research agency Family Kids & Youth and was formerly a director at GfKNOP. Barbie completed her PhD in child and adolescent psychosocial development at the University of Cambridge, Faculty of Education, where her published research has looked at early adolescents' use of digital media. She taught postgraduate students at the faculty for five years. She is a trained child therapist and has worked with young offenders and in secondary schools in Tower Hamlets. A fellow of the Market Research Society (MRS), Barbie regularly writes articles and gives papers at international conferences, and has appeared on TV and radio, commenting on youth research.

Justin Cooke

Justin studied drama at the University of Manchester, majoring in quasi-theatrical leisure and computers as theatre. After graduating, he worked for the BBC, Universal Music and United News and Media before co-founding the global digital agency Fortune Cookie, which he sold to WPP in 2012. He was the chair of the British Interactive Media Association from 2009–2013. He is now chairman of Big Clever Learning, a private-equity backed business focused on acquiring, developing and building the next generation of digital education brands, a venture partner at VC Northzone, a non-executive director of FutureLearn and on the digital advisory board of 10 Downing Street and The British Museum. *Wired* magazine listed him in its top 100 and in 2013 he was inducted into the British Digital Hall of Fame.

Frank Cottrell Boyce

Frank Cottrell Boyce started his career as a staff writer on *Brookside*, set in Frank's native Merseyside. His career has been peppered with awards – highlights include the Academy-Award nominated *Hilary and Jackie*, and his six collaborations with acclaimed director Michael Winterbottom, including *24 Hour Party People* and *A Cock and Bull Story*. His first book for children *Millions* (2003) won the CILIP Carnegie medal and was turned into a movie directed by Danny Boyle. *Framed*, Frank's second novel, was nominated for the Carnegie Medal, the Whitbread Award and the *Guardian* Prize and his third, *Cosmic*, was short listed for the *Guardian* Prize and the inaugural Roald Dahl Funny Prize. *Chitty Chitty Bang Bang Flies Again*, released in 2011, was also shortlisted for the Roald Dahl Funny Prize. Danny Boyle asked Frank to be part of the creative team for the Opening Ceremony of the London 2012 Olympics. Frank worked on the project for two years as the official scriptwriter. When the ceremony was broadcast to an estimated global audience of one billion people, it was met with an overwhelmingly positive reaction, its place in history assured by its bonkers, enthusiastic and incredibly British sensibility.

Joshua Davidson

Joshua Davidson is the co-founder and managing director of Wonky Star Ltd. creators of the magical Night Zookeeper website. Night Zookeeper inspires children to write, draw and be creative online. Joshua is a passionate public speaker on games, education and creativity. He has spoken at many international conferences including MipJunior, Apps World, FutureBook, Children's Media Conference, London Book Fair and the Arab Publishing Conference. Additionally, he is regularly interviewed across news stations such as the BBC for his views on education, creativity and innovations in technology.

Stuart Dredge

Stuart Dredge is a UK-based journalist who writes for *The Guardian, The Observer, The Week Jr* and *Music Ally*. He also runs the Apps Playground website and YouTube channel.

Angela Ferreira

Angela's background is in television production. She trained at CBBC before leaving the BBC as an executive producer and joining Channel 4 as a commissioner. She is now a freelance producer, consultant and trainer. During her time at BBC Children's, Angela worked across the entire spectrum of programmes including Saturday morning live shows and she directed *Bodger and Badger* and *Blue Peter*. Her subsequent roles have included working as series producer on the weekly trendsetting show *The O Zone* for BBC Music and Entertainment, and high profile live-event TV such as *Glastonbury*, *The MOBO Awards*, *Big Brother*, *Notting Hill Carnival Live* and *The*

Isle of Wight Festival. Angela has also produced events for private clients in New York, Switzerland, Belgium and across the UK and has regularly worked with politicians, international government civil servants and NGOs.

Angela has wide experience across media, including appearing as a host and pundit on live radio and TV, and she has spoken about gender stereotyping and diversity in children's TV on various panels. She was also part of the working group that successfully campaigned to have a commitment to diversity enshrined in the BBC Charter.

Angela teaches at The National Film & Television School and sits on their TV Advisory Board, and she is on the Diversity Committee for the Royal Television Society and the Executive Committee of The Children's Media Foundation. She is also a governor at The BRIT School.

Lucy Gill

Lucy is a user-experience specialist and an expert in children's apps and digital toys. She spent ten years as a principal researcher at leading UX agency Serco ExperienceLab before joining Fundamentally Children as a director, creating the Good App Guide and establishing their user-testing services. Lucy now works as an independent consultant/researcher supporting companies in the development and marketing of children's apps, from start-ups to large multinationals. She also remains an active associate for Fundamentally Children.

During her career, Lucy has worked to support product development for companies including McDonalds, BBC, BSkyB, Virgin Media, Channel 4, O2, T-Mobile, Lovefilm and the British Council.

Dr Amanda Gummer

Amanda has over 20 years' experience working with children and families. Widely considered the go-to expert on play, toys and child development, Amanda combines her theoretical knowledge with a refreshingly pragmatic approach to family life that resonates both with parents and professionals. Her book *Play* was published in May 2015 and has already been translated into two different languages. Amanda is regularly in the media and continues to take an active role in research. She is often involved in government policy around children's issues and is a member of two All Party Parliamentary Groups. Amanda ran the research consultancy FUNdamentals for ten

years before combining that with the Good Toy Guide and the Good App Guide to create Fundamentally Children, the UK's leading source of expert, independent advice on child development and play, supporting children's industries with research, insight and endorsement.

Jon Hancock

A BAFTA-winning series producer, Jon spent 15 years at BBC Children's, working across all genres and on iconic shows such as *Blue Peter*, *Short Change* and *Sportsround*. For CBeebies, he created and produced hit in-house shows including *Mr Bloom's Nursery* and *Swashbuckle* and has also produced the last three top-rated CBeebies Christmas productions. Now co-founder of Three Arrows Media, a Manchester-based production house specializing in live-action children's content, Jon is passionate about entertaining, engaging and enriching audiences worldwide.

Derek Holder

David is very much a newcomer to the animation industry – he was involved in IT and telecoms for 20 years and spent the last four years running a small telecoms company, where he learned valuable SEO skills. He is now approaching his fifth year running the Little Baby Bum YouTube channel, and he and his team have grown it to become the number one educational channel in the world. The next five years will see them broadening their horizons and launching multiple products, ranging from magazine and books to toys and clothes.

Anna Home, O.B.E.

Anna is chair of the CMF Board and a founding patron of the organization. Anna joined BBC radio in 1960 and started in children's television in 1964 where she worked as a researcher, then director, producer and executive producer, latterly specialising in children's drama. She started *Grange Hill*, the controversial school series. From 1981–86 she worked at the ITV company TVS where she was deputy director of programmes. In 1986 she returned to the BBC as head of children's programmes responsible for all children's output. She revived the Sunday teatime classic dramas and one of her last decisions before retiring was to commission *Teletubbies*. After retiring from the BBC, Anna was chief executive of the Children's Film & Television Foundation until it merged into CMF in 2012.

Anna has won many awards including a BAFTA lifetime achievement award. She was the first chair of the BAFTA Children's Committee, has chaired both the EBU Children's and Youth Working Group and the Prix Jeunesse International Advisory Board. Anna was the chair of the Save Kids' TV Campaign Executive Committee and the Showcomotion Children's Media Conference. She now chairs the board of the Children's Media Conference, and is a board member of Screen South.

Oli Hyatt

Oli Hyatt has been creative director at Blue-Zoo Animation for 15 years, as well as being the chair of Animation UK. Hits from Blue-Zoo include Nick Jr's *Olive the*

Ostrich and *Digby Dragon* and *Alphablocks* and *Tree Fu Tom* for CBeebies.

His work for Animation UK sees him split his time between meetings at Westminster on the Creative Sector Advisory Group and the Creative Skillset committee, and selling in the tax break overseas with the help of Film London, the BFI and UKTI.

Siwan Jobbins

Siwan Jobbins is an experienced animation and mixed-media producer. While at S4C, she was executive producer on the stop-frame series *Fireman Sam* and *Hana's Helpline*. More recently, she developed and brokered *Abadas*, the first co-production between S4C, RTÉ and Cbeebies. She has developed and produced several pre-school series for S4C and works regularly for BBC Bitesize, including developing and producing content to support KS3 history and the GCSE Welsh curriculum. Siwan has worked on several in-house CBBC projects including producing the online portal, My Toons. She is currently project manager on ANIM8 and works as one of the producers on series two of *Danger Mouse*.

Charlotte Jones

Charlotte Jones is senior research executive at Optimisa Research. During her time at Optimisa she has been involved in a wide variety of market research projects and media projects, from more explorative pieces looking at needs and future direction to more tactical product/concept testing and immersive meet-the-audience sessions. She has an interest in media and communications research and research with young people, particularly their media use and behaviour online, concept understanding and awareness, needs/wants and attribution. She has worked on many projects, from mega-workshops to bedroom hangouts, speaking to 5–21 year olds and the people involved in their lives, such as parents, siblings and carers. She is a member of the Market Research Society.

David Kleeman

Strategist, analyst, author, speaker and connector — for over a quarter of a century, David Kleeman has led the children's media industry in exploring big questions about the future of children's play, learning and media use. Kleeman is currently senior vice president of global trends for Dubit, a strategy/research consultancy and digital studio based in Leeds. He began this work as long-time president of the American Center for Children and Media.

Kleeman serves on the Television Academy Board of Governors, is advisory board chair to the international children's TV festival Prix Jeunesse and a board member of the National Association for Media Literacy Education. He was a 2013 senior fellow of the Fred Rogers Center and 2014 Pioneer Award recipient from Kids@Play Interactive.

Trevor Klein

Trevor is a freelance digital strategist and producer. He works with creative companies to devise and deliver great digital projects for children and young people. Last year, he was the interactive producer for comedy drama *Secret Life of Boys* at Zodiak Kids Studios and before that he produced the BAFTA-nominated educational coding game *The Doctor and the Dalek*. Prior

to going freelance, Trevor was head of development for digital at Somethin' Else, pitching and making award-winning apps, games and interactive stories for brands, broadcasters, museums and publishers. He has also worked at the BBC producing cross-platform projects for 12–16s.

Ray Maguire

Ray has 30 years' experience as a digital technology professional, and his diverse career has had a significant impact on digital technology in the arts, games industry, and now education. He originally trained as an avionics engineer at British Airways and first applied his engineering and electronics skills to his love of film and theatre – he formed Fast Forward Video Productions, which ran the groundbreaking video installations on the West End musical *Chess* in the mid-80s, one of the first theatre productions to incorporate multimedia into a stage show using video walls. Ray then entered the burgeoning games industry at Virgin Mastertronic and with the formation of SEGA UK, he helped introduce the Mega Drive and the world of Sonic the Hedgehog to UK gamers. Ray joined Sony Electronic Publishing Limited in 1993 as director of

sales for Europe. Sony Computer Entertainment was formed in 1994 and Ray became managing director of SCE(UK) to manage the launch of PlayStation. Ultimately, as senior vice president and managing director, Ray oversaw the sales and marketing activities for UK, Ireland, Nordic and Benelux. During the 18 years of running the PlayStation business through the launches of PS2 and PS3 and countless groundbreaking games, Ray instigated many education outreach programs, and it was this that prompted him to become a founding partner in Digital Learning Delivery. DLD strives to demystify the use of video in schools with its cloud based SchoolVID platform. Ray serves on Power To The Pixel advisory board, the CMC advisory board and the BAFTA Games Committee (which he chaired from 2008 to 2012).

Dr Anna Potter

Dr Anna Potter is a Discovery Early Career Research Award (DECRA) fellow and senior lecturer in screen and media studies at the University of the Sunshine Coast in Australia. She is currently working on a three-year grant-funded project examining the effects of media globalization on the production and distribution of children's television. Her book *Creativity, Culture and Commerce: Producing Australian Children's Television with Public Value* was published in 2015. Prior to moving to Australia and becoming an academic, Anna worked for BSkyB in the UK.

Peter Robinson

Peter is an experienced consultant, specializing in new technology, kids' entertainment, heritage kid brands, education and ethical marketing to kids. Wherever possible, he screws all those things together. In his role at Dubit he has developed a firm knowledge of young people, their attitudes and behaviour, particularly focusing on their media consumption and how that is evolving. Peter is a regular speaker at research and kids' entertainment conferences on topics such as emerging technology, social media, video consumption, entertainment brand strategy and children's media habits more broadly.

Kath Shackleton

Kath Shackleton is producer of Fettle Animation, a multi-award winning 2D Studio based in Marsden, near Huddersfield in West Yorkshire. She runs her company with partner Zane Whittingham, an animator with over 25 years' experience. They produce character animation for broadcast, web and digital devices. Their animated documentary series *Children of the Holocaust*, made with BBC Learning, won the Japan Prize Special Jury Prize, the first Sandford St Martin's Children's Awards, two RTS Yorkshire Awards and was nominated for a Children's BAFTA.

They have worked twice on the Children's ITV's BAFTA and Kidscreen Award-winning Share a Story project and have produced Shakespeare in Shorts for BBC Learning, which condenses six Shakespeare plays into three-minute rap-inspired pop songs.

They also create a range of shortform content for BBC, CITV, museums, music producers, businesses and charities. www.fettleanimation.com

Kara Smith

Kara Smith is a Bermudian/British screenwriter and filmmaker living in London. Since graduating from Westminster University's MA Screenwriting Program, her work has garnered several international awards, including a nomination for the International Emmy Peter Ustinov Award, Best International Screenplay at Rhode Island International Film Festival, Best Screenplay at Miami International Sci Fi Film Festival, Grand Prize winner of Hollywood Screenplay Contest and Park Avenue winner of New York Screenplay Contest. Kara has written for *Rastamouse*, *Spot Bots* and *Show Me Show Me* and is currently working on a new live-action children's show. Her directorial debut, short film *Blotter*, screened at the 2015 Cannes International Film Festival and was selected for the 2015 Reykjavik International Film Festival Talent Lab. In March 2016, Kara's debut feature documentary *The Berkeley Project* premiered at the Bermuda International Film Festival.

Alison Stewart

Alison has worked in children's media production for most of her career, first at the BBC and later as a freelance producer, director, scriptwriter and lyricist. She later returned to the BBC as executive producer in CBeebies Production, and moved to her current position six years ago. CBeebies is the BBC's pre-school channel, making mixed genre content for children from 0–6 years. Alison leads a team that creates, develops and produces TV, online, mobile and radio content for the channel, both for the UK audience and for the international market via co-productions.

Claire Stocks

Claire Stocks is head of interactive at BBC Children's, where she runs the digital editorial team and leads the strategic development of digital services and experiences for kids. She joined in January 2015 from BBC Sport where she was digital development editor, one of the senior figures running the Interactive team and platforms. Claire worked in a variety of roles within BBC Sport, including planning and delivering the digital coverage of the London Olympics, leading the streaming and red button team and launching Get Inspired, the BBC's participation initiative. A graduate of Aberdeen University's politics and international relations department and the University of Central Lancashire's postgraduate journalism centre, Claire began her career in regional newspapers – initially at the *North West Daily Mail* in Barrow-in-Furness and then the *Daily Post* and *Echo* in Liverpool. She joined the BBC in 1999 to move into digital content.

Juliet Tzabar

Juliet is managing director at Plug-in Media and has worked in digital media for over 12 years. Following an early career in the art department of television dramas, Juliet moved into digital media in 2000, where she has specialized in delivering interactive projects with a broadcast tie-in for children and their families. Juliet joined Plug-in Media in 2007 and has overseen the company's growth and success, establishing it as one of the UK's leading digital agencies. She takes an executive producer role on many of the company's projects, including the BAFTA-winning *Big and Small* and *Zingzillas*. More recently, Juliet has been overseeing the company's move into original IP development.

Lindsay Watson

Lindsay Watson is a children's animation producer based in London. She got her first "proper job" at kids TV distributor Cake Entertainment in 2008. In 2010 she moved to Cameron Mackintosh as head of digital, working on *Les Miserábles* and *Phantom of the Opera*. In 2012 Lindsay worked as animation consultant for The International VFX Hub in Bournemouth. In 2013 she launched Animated Women UK, a volunteer organization with five key aims: mentoring, networking, showcasing, recruitment and education (www. animatedwomenuk.com).

Lindsay obtained a masters in professional media practice, focused on animation management, from Bournemouth University in 2015. While studying, she was Toon Boom's head of UK business development and sales.

Lindsay founded CANUK Productions in 2013, a private consultancy firm dealing specifically with Canadian/British co-production of animated children's TV series (www.canukproductions. com).

Alice Webb

Alice took up her role as director of BBC Children's in March 2015 after a decade at the BBC. Alice is responsible for the creative and strategic direction of the BBC's children's services and is responsible for the UK's two most popular networks for youngest audiences, CBeebies and CBBC. In her former role as chief operating officer (COO) of BBC England, Alice was responsible for overseeing all aspects of technology, people, workspace, migration and ways of working across the BBC sites in Salford, Bristol and Birmingham. Before joining the BBC Alice was at PA Consulting Group for five years where she worked with organizations including Orange, The Cabinet Office, Reuters and Deutsche Bank. Alice is a Trustee of the Greater Manchester Art Centre (Home) and is a member of the Greater Manchester Business Leadership Council.

Steve Wynne

Steve Wynne is an award-winning creative with over 20 years of production experience in content and television for broadcasters and networks across the globe. He produced ITV's RTS & BAFTA-winning series *SMTV:Live* and *CD:UK* and Disney Channel's BAFTA-winning *Disney Channel Kids Awards* before joining Warner Brothers International Television as director of production in 2005, where he was responsible for the development anf production of all WB television formats created outside the US. In 2007, Steve set up Rival Media, producing primetime factual, features, entertainment and children's series for UK, US and international networks. Hit shows included *Rooftop Rainforest* (Sky 1), *Don't Tell The Bride* (Discovery Networks International), *The Shrinks* (RTE) and *Mission Beach* (BBC2). After taking Rival to a multimillion-pound business from a standing start, Steve launched Pretzel TV in 2013. Pretzel TV received a BAFTA nomination for Independent Production Company of the Year in 2015. The company is currently working on 40+ episodes of the *CBBC Official Chart Show* (CBBC), *Animals Like Us* (Cartoon Network) and a new entertainment series soon to be announced. Steve is dad to three monkeys, likes to write letters of complaint and collects radio jingles.

Angela Young

Angela is passionate about storytelling and engaging young audiences with music and the performing arts. As a multi-camera director, Angela has many years of experience working in both BBC Music and Arts and BBC Children's.

As a producer, Angela has been responsible for the CBeebies and Northern Ballet collaborations, creating Easter events with television, interactive and radio content. Her first 40-minute special for CBeebies, *Ugly Duckling*, won the Children's BAFTA for best pre-school live action. As well as creating one-off specials such as the CBeebies Prom, Angela was the series producer for series nine of *Something Special* and *Old Jack's Boat* spin-off series *Rockpool Tales*.

www.ingramcontent.com/pod-product-compliance
Lightning Source LLC
Chambersburg PA
CBHW040927050426

42334CB00062B/3261